"Full of inspiring Scripture and engaging illustrations from both God's Word and everyday life, *Big Steps, Little Steps* provides invaluable insights into our relationship with our loving heavenly Father."

— AARON SHUST, American contemporary Christian music artist. GMA Dove Awards: 2007 Songwriter of the Year

"Filled with biblical truth and real-life examples of Christians who walked before us and some walking beside us, *Big Steps, Little Steps* will be your daily companion and encouragement on the journey called life. M. Esther Lovejoy writes from her heart to ours, always pointing to the One who invites us to "Follow Me." The devotions are short, strong, and perfect to read before your toes touch the floor running each morning."

— ELAINE W. MILLER, International speaker and author of four books including, *We All Married Idiots* and *Praise the Lord and Pass the Chemo*

"*Big Steps, Little Steps* is a beautifully written devotional book that offers scriptural truths and practical everyday examples for our lifelong adventure with God! One that leads us to joy in our relationship with Him as we experience and practice His presence in our own personal realities. Arranged by topics rather than by days or weeks, you will enjoy the freedom it brings to pick up and read as the Holy Spirit leads you!"

— ANITA KEAGY, JoyShop Ministries

"It has been a privilege and honor to work with Esther Lovejoy over the last several years through her radio blog that airs on Saturday afternoons on WPGM. Her short feature is scripturally based but also incorporates things from everyday life. She also talks about the importance of walking with the Lord, letting Him lead you in your daily life, and drawing your strength from Him. I am sure that her book will minister to those who read it, in the same way that it has ministered to those who have heard her short feature program."

— DEANNA FORCE, Operations Manager WPGM-WBGM radio

"In *Big Steps, Little Steps* readers will find inspiration and encouragement. Esther Lovejoy's wise and gentle spirit, which helped to guide my wife many years ago, shows up fully in this devotional. Her obvious high reverence for our heavenly Father shines through each page. Her desire for her readers to sense, feel, and live fully captivated by the love of our God also shines through. Readers will enjoy this walk and know they have moved forward."

— DR. RON BELSTERLING, Author of *A Defense of Youth Ministry*, Professor, Youth and Young Adult Ministry Program Director, Lancaster Bible College

BIG STEPS
LITTLE STEPS
Moving forward in our walk with God

M. ESTHER LOVEJOY

ST JOSEPH, MISSOURI USA

To Peter
I am so thankful for the twenty-one years
I was blessed to walk this journey with you.

Contents

9

Acknowledgments

On the front cover of this book is my name as the author. But there are so many other names not listed on the front cover that were also a big part of bringing this book into being.

My thanks to *Dave Fessenden*, my agent and friend. I am so grateful for your commitment to finding the right publisher for *Big Steps, Little Steps*. And you did! When I first came to CrossRiver Media, I had no idea I would find so much more than a publisher. I found friends who prayed for me, loved me, encouraged me…and published my book.

Thank you, *Tami*. You have gone way beyond the job description of a good publisher and become a cherished friend.

Thank you, *Deb*, for your patient editing and help in so many other practical ways. You've been such a wonderful and much-needed friend and help.

And to CrossRiver's encourager and cheerleader, *DeeDee*: What a blessing you've been as you've continually encouraged me through the process and prayed for me during some rough days.

My husband *Peter* passed away before he could see this book in print. But, as always, he was my biggest encourager and support. He believed I could and should write and kept after me to use the gift he believed God had given me. I'm so thankful for that encouragement.

Introduction

Master storyteller and veterinarian James Herriot relates a conversation with one of the farmers he served in a remote area of the Yorkshire Dales. The farmer was accustomed to walking with long even strides through his fields or along country roads without being jostled and pushed by other people. On one occasion, after a trip to the city, he complained to Herriot that he found it difficult to walk. "There were that many people about," he explained. "I 'ad to take big steps and little 'uns, then big steps and little 'uns again.'"

That's often a good description of our spiritual walk. We're jostled about by the demands and worries of life; we're pushed and shoved by the world around us and our walk becomes one of "big steps and little 'uns." The psalmist may have been facing the same frustration when he prayed for God to enlarge his steps (Psalm 18:36 KJV).

Big Steps, Little Steps is comprised of devotional readings to encourage those steps of faith, whether "big 'uns or little 'uns." In these pages you'll find scriptural truths applied in a practical way to our daily walk with God. My prayer is God will use them to enlarge your steps in your walk with Him.

Jeremiah reminds us "it is not in man who walks to direct his steps" (Jeremiah 10:23). God has promised to guide us, whether our steps are large or small. Both lead us forward. Both lead to Him.

Walking with Greatness

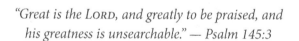

"Great is the Lord, and greatly to be praised, and his greatness is unsearchable." — Psalm 145:3

You Can't Exaggerate God

"There is none like you, O Lᴏʀᴅ;
you are great." — Jeremiah 10:6

My dad's gentle but humorous way of correcting his children when he felt we were embellishing the truth was to say, "For the millionth time, don't exaggerate!" We got the message, even if he had to remind us a million times.

Did you know you can't exaggerate God? What a wonderful truth. The dictionary says to exaggerate is to represent something as greater than is actually the case, but God simply can't be represented as anything greater than He truly is.

Think of Him in the highest and most glorious way possible, and He is higher and more glorious. Stretch your mind to its full limit to imagine the vastness of His power, and He is even more powerful. Try to envision the depth and breadth and height of a love that is absolutely pure and perfect, and His love is broader and higher and deeper still. And His holiness is not only beyond comprehension, it is also beyond any attempt to express it.

Job describes the amazing works of God and then says, "how small a whisper we hear of him!" (Job 26:14b). All our thoughts about God are based on those whispers—whispers we find in Scripture, whispers when He meets with us in prayer, whispers when we look at creation. Even those whispers are enough to bring us to our knees in humble worship.

I love that God is beyond my wildest imagination, my profoundest thoughts, and my deepest longings. He is greater, higher, holier, wiser, and (thankfully) more loving than my mind can conceive. He is all I need a God for, and even if I say it a million times, it's still gloriously true—He simply cannot be exaggerated!

Prayer

Dear great and glorious God: How wonderful to walk with a God who is beyond the scope of our greatest thoughts. I love that You are so gloriously above anything we can think or imagine. What we know about You brings us to our knees in worship, and those are just whispers of who You are. We bow in awe of Your greatness. Amen.

An Endless Journey

"'To whom will you compare me? Or who is my equal?' says the Holy One." — Isaiah 40:25 (NIV)

I love the vastness of God. He has no edges—no boundaries or borders. There is no limit to Him. We can know Him (how amazing!), but we can never know all of Him. What we know about God—His power, His holiness, His majesty—is enough to bring us to our knees in humble adoration and worship. But what should bring us absolutely prostrate before Him is all that remains mysterious and unknown. All that sets Him apart as God.

Imagine if someone came upon the Grand Canyon and declared, "I have just found the Grand Canyon!" and then turned around and went home. Think of all they would have missed. Imagine all that was yet to be discovered. They did find the Grand Canyon, but finding it was just the beginning of their journey. There were still endless parts yet to be explored.

Where this illustration falls short is that, even with its vastness, there is an end to the Grand Canyon, but there is no end to God! Tozer states, "To have found God and still to pursue Him is the soul's paradox of love." Usually when something is found, the search is over, but not so with the Almighty. To find Him is just the beginning.

There are aspects of God that are incomprehensible, aspects of His nature beyond our finite ability to grasp. And that's part of the joy of seeking Him. There simply is no end. There's no point at which we've arrived and can claim full understanding of God. It's an ongoing and soul-satisfying quest. To know God is to love and worship Him. To love and worship Him is to long to know Him better. And on and on goes this glorious and endless journey!

Prayer

Dear great and glorious God: Thank you for the amazing privilege of knowing You. Job reminds us that what we know of You now is "but the outer fringe" of Your works. One of the joys of heaven will be spending eternity discovering more and more of the wonders of who You are. It truly is an endless journey. Amen.

The Sovereign God

"The LORD will reign forever and ever." — Exodus 15:18

We live in a very unsettled world with unrest between nations and unrest within the borders of many nations. We live with the threat of war and with missiles aimed in our direction. Even our own country is experiencing changes that can't help but be alarming to us as Christians.

In the midst of all of this, I find tremendous comfort and hope in the absolute sovereignty of God. Psalm 47:8 declares "God reigns over the nations." And I love the reminder in Psalm 33 that "the LORD foils the plans of the nations; he thwarts the purposes of the peoples. But the plans of the LORD stand firm forever, the purposes of his heart through all generations" (vv. 10–11 NIV).

What a wonderful reminder during unsettled days. God is in charge! He is the sovereign ruler over all! The world situation may be frightening, the changes we see in our own nation may be alarming, but God's plans will stand firm forever—the purposes of His loving heart will remain unchanged through all generations. We have the assurance that "for those who love God all things work together for good" (Romans 8:28). God isn't standing idly by. He is weaving all these threads together

21

for His purposes. Nothing that happens today will alter the end of the story God has already written.

The familiar words of Jeremiah 29:11 remind us that God's plans are "for welfare and not for evil, to give…a future and a hope." That future includes a kingdom where we will live with Him for all eternity, where there will be no unrest without or within. But best of all, a kingdom where He will reign in undisputed, absolute sovereignty forever and ever!

Prayer

Dear Father: I find great comfort in Your sovereignty. Nothing is a surprise to You and nothing will thwart Your purposes from being fulfilled. I love this truth for my own life, for our nation, and for the world. Thank You for letting us know the ending ahead of time. That helps. Amen.

The Whole God

"God said to Moses, 'I AM WHO I AM.'" — *Exodus 3:14*

When my granddaughter was little, she and her friend were sitting on the floor building things out of those chunky pre-school Lego blocks. After a few minutes of great concentration, her friend looked at what she had made and said proudly, "Look! I made Jesus." Tanner, glancing at her own Lego creation (which was considerably larger) said, "Well, I made the whole God!" Those of us watching couldn't help but laugh at this innocent exchange.

I can't help wonder if we aren't guilty of occasionally doing the same thing. We pick up the attributes and characteristics of God we like, or are comfortable with, stack them together and then declare it to be "the whole God!"

But God can't be formed by us—by our own thoughts or preferences. We can't build Him to be how we would like Him to be. We can't pick up His love and grace and leave out His justice and wrath. His attributes are an amazing and perfect blend. There is perfect unity in all He is. And whether we realize it or not, we really do need a God with every one of His characteristics. God is perfect just as He is.

The truth of the matter is we simply can't improve on God.

He is so much greater than anything we could put together. Even our grandest and most profound thoughts couldn't construct a perfect god sufficient for all our needs. To leave out some of His characteristics we find difficult or unsettling is like stacking together chunky Legos and thinking we have the whole god. The true God is made up of a perfect blend of attributes that make Him worthy of our worship. Don't build your own God. Ask the true God to reveal all of Himself to you. He's better than anything you can imagine!

Prayer

Dear Holy God: The fact we don't always understand you is simply a reflection of our limited understanding and Your greatness. You are perfect. We need You to be exactly as You are. Forgive us for trying to remake You into a god we find more comfortable and understandable. It would be to our loss if You were anything other than the great "I Am!" Amen.

Big Bang or Mighty God?

"He who brings out the starry host one by one and calls forth each of them by name." — Isaiah 40:26b NIV

Recently my husband and I were watching a news program reporting on some new technology that reveals details of space never before seen. These radio telescopes have been set up on a plateau in Chile where the geography and altitude offer one of the clearest views of the sky found on Earth. And they are revealing some truly amazing things, things never seen before even by powerful telescopes or satellites.

As we watched, we were awed by the display of stars. I couldn't help but think of the words of Psalm 19:1, "The heavens declare the glory of God, and the sky above proclaims his handiwork." But apparently the scientists weren't listening to the message the sky and stars were declaring about the glory of God. In fact, they seemed to get an entirely different message. They shared with great pride they were closer than ever to actually finding the big bang, the explosion that began the universe.

How sad! They were gazing at one of the most awesome displays of God's creative power. They were seeing details of the universe never seen before—details displaying order and perfection. But they preferred to find origin in chaos rather than in a Creator. They missed the message of the stars.

I think when we, as God's children, look up into a starry sky at night, we may not see all that those scientists can see. We may not have the advantage of the latest equipment and technology, but we do have the wonder and joy and knowing what those stars declare. There is a great and awesome Creator who put those stars in place and knows each one by name. Even with my limited view, I like what I see a lot better. Even to the naked eye, the heavens really do declare the glory of our God!

Prayer

Dear awesome and mighty God: We see evidence of Your creative power all around us whether we look up at the vast universe or down at a tiny flower. We see Your fingerprints and personal touch all over creation. And You saw it was good and we agree. We bow in humble admiration at the work of Your hands. Amen.

Seven Wonderful Words

"Behold, I am the Lord, the God of all flesh.
Is anything too hard for me?" — Jeremiah 32:27

H ave you ever had a dream that left you with a very uncomfortable feeling, and then to make it worse, you couldn't remember the dream when you woke up? That happened to a very powerful king in the Bible named Nebuchadnezzar. Scripture tells us he was very troubled and couldn't sleep. He immediately called in all the wise men and magicians of the kingdom and demanded they not only interpret his dream, but that they tell him what the dream was—not an easy assignment! And, as it turned out, one they couldn't accomplish.

This only added to the king's frustration, and he decided to take out his frustration by having them all killed. But then Daniel stepped in. I love how Daniel gently points out the obvious to Nebuchadnezzar. He tells the king what he's asked truly is impossible. No one can do this. But then Daniel adds these seven wonderful words to this impossible situation—"but there is a God in heaven" (Daniel 2:28). Daniel tells King Nebuchadnezzar there is a God who is greater than his problem.

I love those seven words. I love the hope they bring to any impossible situation. What about you? Are you facing something today for which there seems to be no human solution? Are you in the middle of circumstances for which there is no answer no matter which way you turn? For you today, there are these same seven wonderful words, "but there is a God in heaven"—a God who is greater than any of your problems and One who can still bring hope to impossible situations.

Prayer

Dear mighty God: These men were asked to do the impossible. We sometimes face situations that seem impossible. There are no easy answers. There seems to be no hope. And Daniel's answer is still true for us today. For whatever we face, there is still that same God in heaven. Thank You for those seven wonderful words. Amen.

Two Branches, One River

"Humble yourselves, therefore, under the mighty hand of God, so that at the proper time he may exalt you." — 1 Peter 5:6

We were traveling over a bridge the other day, and I commented on the beauty of the river as we passed over it. Much to my surprise, we immediately crossed over a second river while on the same bridge. My husband saw my puzzled look and explained those were two branches of the same river and just down the road they became one.

God has been teaching me in two specific areas recently. I thought they were two separate truths, but as I've followed them, I've discovered they are actually two branches of the same river as God has shown me the wonderful connection between these two truths.

The first branch is fearing God. It is very important to realize God is so far beyond us that our response must be one of reverence and awe when we approach Him.

The other branch of the river has come through re-reading Andrew Murray's book on humility. He continually stresses the importance of our nothingness so God can be all. The book has made me long for the reality of this in my own life. Humility is not just a posture I choose to take, but rather my rightful place before God and people.

As I've been responding to God's teaching in these areas, He has brought the two together into one great flowing stream. Humility is the only appropriate response to who God is—to His greatness, to His overwhelming and indescribable purity and holiness, and to His sovereign authority over all of creation. It's not because I'm nothing that I should display humility, but because God is everything! The joy is that humility moves me out of the way so God can be seen in all His greatness and glory.

Prayer

Dear amazing God: I love the reality that humility is simply taking our rightful place before Your greatness. It comes from gazing at You, not by focusing on me. It's not a false sense of nothingness. It's not inferiority. It's actually just a glorious understanding of who I am in light of who You are. Thank You for continuing to teach me. Amen.

Stepping Closer

"Draw near to God,
and He will draw near to you." — James 4:8a

Boldly with Fear and Trembling

"[S]ince we have confidence to enter the Most
Holy Place by the blood of Jesus...let us draw
near to God." — Hebrews 10:19, 22 NIV

The Christian life is marked by paradox. We gain our life by losing it. We're made strong through our weakness. We're lifted up by humbling ourselves.

Our access to God is also marked by paradox. In Jeremiah 5:22, God Himself asks, "Do you not fear me?" To add emphasis to that question, He adds, "Do you not tremble before me?" The obvious response is, "Yes!" I think if God were to reveal Himself in all His majesty, we wouldn't need to be instructed to respond in fear and trembling. I suspect that would be our involuntary and appropriate response. And yet the writer of Hebrews urges us to come boldly, reminding us of the joyous access that is ours, to the throne of the Almighty.

Isaiah reveals this same paradox: "But the LORD of hosts, him you shall honor as holy. Let him be your fear, and let him be your dread. And he will become a sanctuary" (Isaiah 8:13–14a). The very One we are to fear offers Himself as our safe place.

A clear image of this is found in *The Lion, the Witch, and the Wardrobe* by C. S. Lewis. As Lucy is about to meet the magnificent lion, Aslan, she asks if he's safe. Mr. Beaver sums up the paradox simply by stating of course Aslan isn't safe, but he is good. She could meet him boldly, but with fear and trembling.

We must never forget God is God. Trembling is an appropriate response. But the wonderful news is God's own Son purchased the right and privilege for us to come into His presence with boldness. It's the freedom of burying our face in Aslan's mane while never forgetting he's a fierce lion. What a blessed paradox!

Prayer

Almighty and Holy God: May our freedom to step boldly into Your presence always be coupled with an appropriate sense of awe and reverence. You are God. Never let us forget apart from Your Son we would never dare to approach You. Thank You for the privilege of boldness. Amen.

Don't Waste Your Time

"The LORD is near to all who call on him." — Psalm 145:18a

Trying to figure God out is a waste of time; getting to know Him never is." Those words were spoken by a close friend of mine at a very difficult time in her life. Both of her parents were missing. Kathy's mother was a diabetic and both parents suffered from Alzheimer's. There were many anxious days of waiting and worrying (hoping for the best, fearing the worst), but finally when hoping for the best became unrealistic, the remains of Kathy's parents were discovered. It was in these circumstances she uttered those deeply significant words.

Kathy learned that trying to figure God out brought her no comfort—only confusion. Scripture makes it clear His ways aren't our ways. In fact, it goes on to say His ways—even His unexplainable ways—are higher or superior to ours. And so, Kathy chose instead to trust God's heart and to draw close to Him—to learn to know Him better during those dark days of grief and confusion. And for Kathy, that was time well spent.

What about you? Are you trying to figure out God, trying to find an explanation for what He's doing or allowing in your life? May I encourage you to listen to Kathy's wisdom. Don't waste your time trying to come up with answers, to find an explanation for God's ways, but instead, use the circumstances you're in, the difficulty you're facing, as an opportunity to draw near and get to know Him better.

Prayer

Dear sovereign God: There are so many things in life that leave us confused. So many unanswered questions. Sometimes in our frustration or anger, we want to push You away. But it's in choosing to draw near we find something more precious than answers. Help us to remember we know enough about You to trust You for what we don't know. Amen.

The Lost Art of Tarrying

"Be still, and know that I am God." — Psalm 46:10a

I was reading in 1 John the other day and read these words in verse 28 of chapter 2, "And now, little children, abide in Him." John is lovingly encouraging these early Christians in their relationship with Christ. Other versions use the word *continue* or *remain*, but the original Greek word also means "to tarry." I like that thought—tarry in Him. There is such a sense of unhurriedness in the idea of tarrying. The dictionary defines it as "to linger in expectation." It's not an impatient waiting or a restless hanging around, but a quiet remaining, knowing this is not wasted time.

I've been reading a wonderful book entitled, *They Knew Their God*. It's the story of seventeen well-known Christians throughout history. They come from different countries, different periods of time, different cultures, and even different theological positions, but what they all had in common was they had learned to tarry, to linger in expectation in the presence of God.

For most of us, tarrying isn't part of our schedules. We hurriedly rush from one activity to another, convinced we don't have time for stillness. But God asks us—invites us—to tarry in His presence. The songwriter expressed it this way, "and He walks with me and He talks with me, and He tells me I am His own. And the joy we share as we tarry there, none other has ever known." Don't miss out on that joy. Learn to tarry, to linger in expectation in Christ. It will be time well spent.

Prayer

Dear Father: We live in a culture that encourages busyness. Tarrying is not encouraged. We miss out on so much when we don't take the time to be still. The irony is it's in those times of stillness we gain what we need for the busyness. Help us to draw near and linger in expectation in Your wonderful presence. Amen.

Devoted to Nearness

"[I]n your presence there is fullness of joy." — Psalm 16:11b

The Lord asks a thought-provoking question in Jeremiah 30:21. He asks, "who is he who will devote himself to be close to me?" (NIV). I've always been challenged by this question. What about me? Am I one who is "devoted" to being close to God? Not just wanting to but making decisions that reflect that desire.

The Hebrew use of the word *devoted* implies a giving over even to the point of death. In other words, nothing else is of greater importance. Closeness to God becomes my passion, my priority, and my continual pursuit.

I think we see a beautiful illustration of this in the picture of the sparrow in Psalm 84:3. I'm sure other birds flew into the temple on occasion, but this one decided to build her nest there. She didn't want to just flit in and out, she wanted to live there. She *devoted* herself to making it her home.

God invites us to be continually in His presence. The sparrow's choice was evident by her nest. Where is my nest? Where do I live? Am I satisfied to just flit in and out of God's presence, or am I building my home there? Perhaps these are questions we all need to ask. Can we truthfully say, "I will give myself over completely, above all else, to being close to God—to building my nest in His presence?"

The next verse in Psalm 84 says this, "Blessed (happy, fortunate, to be envied) are those who dwell in Your house *and* Your presence; they will be singing Your praises all the day long" (v. 4 AMPC). We look for so many other ways to be happy and blessed, but God offers us this amazing privilege of building our nest in His presence and enjoying the rich rewards of being close to Him.

Prayer

Dear loving God: It's sad You even have to ask that question. It's also sad we don't take full advantage of the amazing privilege You offer us to draw near and live in Your glorious presence. I pray our answer to Your question will always be, "It's me!" Amen.

Potential for Greatness

"You shall love the Lord your God
with all your heart." — Matthew 22:37

I've always wanted to be really good at something. If only I could weave the most intricate fabric, bake the best sticky buns, or produce an amazing quilt. But, above all, I wanted to be the best mother ever—the one whose children would all "arise and call her blessed" (Proverbs 31:28 NIV).

I've enjoyed weaving and quilting, baking and mothering, but have fallen short of being great in any of those areas. And I don't see anything in my near future that suggests greatness in any other accomplishments.

But today I read these words by A. W. Tozer: "The great in the kingdom have always been those who loved God more than others did." Notice he didn't say the great in the church, or in Christianity—that greatness is measured by man. But Tozer declares the potential for greatness that is measured by God and is attainable for each of us. Amy Carmichael encourages us also with the reminder even the least of us can be a lover of God. It doesn't require years of training or education, professional credits, or an impressive resume. It simply requires a heart that longs to return to God some measure of the love He offers to us.

Would you like to experience greatness? Would you like to excel at something that leads to a greatness seen by God alone? Then look for every opportunity to deepen your love for God by spending time with Him. Draw close and get to know Him more, and you'll find it impossible not to love Him more. And the best part is, soon you'll find yourself lost in the only greatness that matters—the greatness of loving God!

Prayer

Dear Father: You have given each of us an opportunity for greatness—the greatness of loving You. As with anything, we don't become great without making it our priority. Lord, help us to spend time with You, to learn to know You better so we will love You more deeply. Amen.

Time for Fellowship

"Mary...sat at the Lord's feet and
listened to his teaching." — Luke 10:39b

Recently I picked up an old copy of *The Deeper Christian Life* by Andrew Murray and was immediately impacted by his opening sentence. "The first and chief need of our Christian life is, Fellowship with God."

Think of all that has changed since those words were first written in 1895. We live in a society that bears little resemblance to Andrew Murray's life at the turn of the century. The culture of today is vastly different due to amazing advances in technology beyond what he could have imagined. The values and philosophies that influence our lives today are also vastly different. And yet, in spite of those differences, these words remain as important and significant as when they were first written over one hundred years ago. They are, quite simply, true.

We probably all agree with this, but do we live our lives as if this were true? Do our days include time for uninterrupted fellowship with the Almighty? I don't mean a quick devotional reading and a hurried listing of our needs and wants to God. It's more than listening to a worship CD on our way to work. Fellowship implies unhurried time in the presence of someone we truly enjoy.

I think it's interesting Christ makes it clear this is what He wants. Christ shares in Revelation 3:21 that He is knocking at our heart's door, waiting to be invited in to eat together, to have fellowship. In New Testament times, eating together often meant reclining over a relaxed and unhurried meal. When was the last time you enjoyed relaxed, unhurried time with the Lord?

I haven't gotten very far in reading *The Deeper Christian Life*. In fact, I haven't gotten past that first sentence. Andrew Murray is absolutely right! My first and chief need, even more than spending time reading his book, is fellowship with God, time to just enjoy His presence.

I'm sure the rest of Andrew Murray's book is excellent, and one of these days I'll get to it. But, in the meantime, I'm learning many of my other needs are met when I make fellowship with God my priority. It's time well spent.

Prayer

Dear loving Father: I think it's hard for us to imagine spending time with us is something You desire. I wonder how often I've left You standing at my heart's door knocking while I've been busy doing other things, often things related to Your Church. Help me to answer Your knock and enjoy the amazing privilege of fellowship with You. There's nothing sweeter. Amen.

Wanna Hear a Secret?

"My sheep hear my voice...and they follow me." — John 10:27

As a small boy, my husband Peter was visiting a family friend affectionately known as Uncle Buster. While they were out walking together, Uncle Buster asked, "Wanna hear a secret?" Peter was thrilled Uncle Buster would share a secret with him and couldn't wait to hear what he had to say. Uncle Buster leaned over and whispered in a tone of utmost importance and secrecy, "There are leprechauns in these woods. If you look carefully, you just might see one." While Peter never did catch a glimpse of a leprechaun, he did come home with a new sense of importance. Uncle Buster had chosen to share this amazing secret with him.

We all feel special when someone chooses to take us into their confidence, when someone is willing to share their heart with us. Scripture tells us in Psalm 25:14 (NIV), "The LORD confides in those who fear him." This amazing truth is repeated in Proverbs 3:32: "but takes the upright into His confidence." Wow! God is willing to take us into His confidence. These verses reveal that God longs for a sense of intimacy and closeness with us that give Him the opportunity to lean over and say, "Wanna hear a secret?"

Think about the significance of those words. Think about the privilege God is offering to us. The Almighty is willing to take us into His confidence. Peter looked up to Uncle Buster and so was impressed with the privilege of hearing his secret. How much more should we be humbled and overwhelmed that the Almighty God is willing to take us into His confidence.

Secrets aren't yelled across a room, but shared with someone who is close enough to hear. Peter heard Uncle Buster's secret because he was walking right beside him. God will share His heart and truth with us when we are willing to spend time in His presence—to walk and talk with Him in close fellowship, close enough for Him to share His secrets.

Prayer

Dear loving Father: I am always amazed and humbled by Your desire for a close relationship with us. We would never dare to initiate such a relationship with a holy God, but You have made full provision for it and full assurance it's Your heart's desire. Thank You that when we draw near, You're willing to confide Your heart to us. We are awed by that privilege. Amen.

Confident Steps

"In quietness and in trust shall be your strength." — Isaiah 30:15c

Roller Coaster Ride Times Two

"For I know the plans I have for you, declares the
LORD, plans for welfare and not for evil, to give
you a future and a hope." — Jeremiah 29:11

I enjoy amusement parks and for me a must-do is the roller coaster. I realize not everyone shares my enthusiasm. After one ride, as we were coming into the gate after the usual exciting twists and drops, the man at the controls looked at us, grinned, and said, "Oh, why not?" as he pushed the lever to send us off for another ride. The woman behind us was not at all pleased with his generosity and screamed, "NOOOO!" Having survived it once, she wasn't at all excited about doing it again.

Not long ago my husband and I found ourselves in an experience that felt much like a roller coaster ride with unexpected twists and turns and sudden drops that took our breath away. It was a tremendous relief when we realized we were approaching the end when suddenly we were off for a second ride. I felt much like that woman as I screamed out to God, "NOOOO!"

But the Lord lovingly taught me some truths about roller coasters. Every twist and turn, every sudden drop, has been carefully designed by an expert. The carts run on tracks engineered for a safe, though perhaps frightening, ride. The drops are never too steep, and the turns will never actually send us over the edge. What seems like an out-of-control ride is actually well-planned with our safety in mind. Best of all, it's designed to come to an end. A roller coaster ride never lasts forever.

What a wonderful reminder! God has engineered every twist and turn or unexpected drop in our lives. He is still in control and will bring us to a safe and expected end—even if it is the second time around.

Prayer

Dear sovereign God: How comforting to know when life seems to be out of control, there is One for whom it holds no surprises. You know every twist and turn and will bring us safely to an expected end. Thank You for engineering life so, even when it's frightening, it is under Your control. Amen.

Who Needs a GPS?

"I will instruct you and teach you in the
way you should go." — Psalm 32:8a

We seldom use our GPS, partly because we don't seem to go anywhere new, but also because we have seen (and been slightly amused at) the frustration of so many GPS users as they've been directed the wrong way, or the long way, and occasionally to the wrong place. (My husband still has a flip phone, which may give you a hint where he is with technology.) I know a church whose correct address when entered in a GPS consistently sends people to the wrong place. Each Sunday the pastor wonders how many visitors are sitting in a parking lot across town.

However, we all have times when we need a GPS for our lives—when we're faced with uncertainty about which direction to take. In those situations, we don't just want directions, we want right directions.

Psalm 18:36 gives us a wonderful visual of God's willingness to guide. In the King James, it says God will *enlarge* our steps. I love the picture of large footprints in front of us that we can't possibly miss. The NIV says God will "provide a broad path." Both of these make it clear God will guide us in an obvious and unmistakable way.

Yesterday my son went hiking and got lost. He found himself in an area where it became very hard to distinguish the trail. It was a great relief to him when, after a couple of hours of wandering and wondering, the path suddenly broadened. He knew then that he was heading in the right direction.

The Lord makes it clear in Jeremiah 10:23 it's really not up to us to direct our own steps. We can't see the path ahead to know which way to take. He offers us His GPS, God's Planned Steps, which are always clear and always right. Now that's a GPS worth having!

Prayer

Dear Father: We are so blessed to have Someone to give us direction. We so often aren't sure of the right path to take and love Your assurance that You will make our next steps clear. You know best. You know what's ahead, and so we trust You to lead. Amen.

Unexpected Company

"And my God will supply every need of yours according to his riches in glory in Christ Jesus." — Philippians 4:19

I enjoy having company. I like getting things ready, planning meals, cooking, and baking delicious desserts, all in preparation for my guests. Unexpected company is another thing. While I'm smiling and welcoming them, I'm mentally going through my refrigerator and pantry trying to come up with a combination of ingredients to make a palatable meal or trying to figure if we have enough to take them out to eat.

Imagine having more than 5,000 show up unexpectedly for a meal. That's what happened to Christ and his disciples. Crowds of people had followed Jesus to a remote area to listen to His teaching. They suddenly became aware they were hungry and needed to eat.

While the disciples were mentally going through the refrigerator and calculating the cost, it says Christ "already had in mind what He was going to do" (John 6:6 NIV). I love those words. There was no panic, no quick mental calculations. He already knew exactly what was needed and how He would respond to the need. The results were that everyone had more than enough.

I also love that His provision came by multiplying the limited resources already available. Who could ever imagine five loaves and two little fish could feed a multitude? So often when faced with an unexpected situation, we find our resources are not enough. God can still take little and bless it and multiply it to meet our need.

I find great comfort in this familiar story. When I face unexpected problems in life, when I am totally unprepared for something that comes my way, Christ has a plan. He is prepared for my need, and already has in mind what He's going to do—and it will be more than enough.

Prayer

Dear loving Father: We are often caught off guard by a problem or need. We find ourselves unprepared and without resources for some unforeseen situation. This story is such a wonderful reminder. You had a plan to feed more than 5,000 people, and You have a plan for whatever comes into my life. What may be unexpected to me, isn't to You. When my resources seem limited, You can bless them and multiply them. You are such a good, good God! Amen.

The Manifest Presence of God

"Now faith is the assurance of things hoped for, the conviction of things not seen." — Hebrews 11:1

What an amazing experience it must have been to live when Jesus walked here on Earth. Imagine the joy of the shepherds to kneel before the baby whose birth had been triumphantly declared by angels. Imagine the privilege of Mary to love and care for God in the flesh. So many knew Him and listened to Him. Others felt the power of His touch as legs were made new and sight was restored. I feel a little jealousy for those who experienced Jesus in person. But I didn't live in those times. I wasn't one of those privileged to see Christ, to hear Him preach, to watch His miracles.

I have, however, been privileged to experience His presence—a sense of the reality of God's manifest presence even when He wasn't seen. I remember a time when a group of teens was praying in the Prayer Chapel at our youth camp and God came and met with us. His presence was so real. I was also privileged to be at Asbury during the great revival that began there and spread to so many other colleges and churches. You could sense the presence of the Almighty as soon as you walked into Hughes Auditorium. There have also been pre-

M. ESTHER LOVEJOY

cious times of personal prayer and worship when God made His presence known and felt.

But the manifest presence of God isn't our usual experience. Often, we pray, sometimes even worship, without a sense of God's presence. What then? Recently God reminded me the only difference between those times is my awareness of Him—not the reality of His presence. He is just as surely there when I don't sense Him as in those wonderful moments when I do. That's faith—the confidence in what isn't seen or felt.

God has promised to be with us. God has promised never, never, never to leave us. And God's presence isn't measured by my sense of His presence, but by the promise of His presence.

I didn't see the baby Jesus. I didn't hear the words of Christ as He taught or healed. Nor do I feel His manifest presence every time I read His Word or pray. But He is no less real. And that truth brings me great "comfort and joy" all year long.

Prayer

Dear Father: Your presence is not dependent on my feelings, but rather on Your promises. You've promised never to leave me. You've promised to be a very present help in trouble. And I rest in Your promises rather than my feelings. Amen.

A Path to the Impossible

"For my thoughts are not your thoughts, neither are your ways my ways." — Isaiah 55:8

One of the most dramatic stories in the Old Testament is the familiar story of the parting of the Red Sea. The Israelites were literally trapped between the Red Sea and the approaching chariots of Pharaoh's army. What was Moses thinking? Why had he led them right into danger? But the truth is Moses hadn't led them to the Red Sea. God had. God had led them on a path that brought them face-to-face with the impossible.

Scripture tells us God took them the long way around to protect them from the Philistines. I doubt they felt much comfort in that as they stood facing the waters of the Red Sea. Moses encouraged them with these words: "Fear not, stand firm, and see the salvation of the LORD, which he will work for you today" (Exodus 14:13). God first led them to an impossible situation, and then did the impossible to save them from that situation.

There are times when we know we've been following the Lord's leading, but we find ourselves in an impossible situation. We see an insurmountable Red Sea in front of us and a fast-approaching army behind us with no sign of escape. Moses' words are just as true for us today as they were for the Israelites. "The LORD will fight for you; you need only to be still" (Exodus 14:14 NIV). We find an echo of that in David's words: "Be still, and know that I am God" (Psalm 46:10).

What happened that day for the Israelites as they began their journey to the Promised Land was more than just the parting of water and a dry path to walk across. God's people saw an amazing display of the power of God. They experienced God's provision and protection. If God had placed them on a path to the possible, they would have missed the miracle. Instead, God led them down a path to the impossible for His glory. And He still does.

Prayer

Dear loving Guide: We don't always understand Your ways. We don't always like the paths You choose for us. Help us remember what You did for Israel You can do for us as a display of Your power for Your glory. Amen.

When There's No Burning Bush

"Blessed are the people…who walk, O LORD,
in the light of your face." — Psalm 89:15

Have you ever wished for a burning bush experience—a time when God would supernaturally appear to give you instructions or directions, a time when God would come and sit beside you and audibly explain His plan and His purposes?

Apparently, even a burning bush isn't always enough. Moses had dramatic evidence of God's leading and call on His life. He was standing in front of a bush that was engulfed in flames, yet the fire did not consume it. But even more, he was standing in front of a bush from which emanated the clear and audible voice of God. That's a pretty clear call and yet Moses still questioned it. His response to God's clear call was, "Who am I that I should go to Pharaoh?" (Exodus 3:11). Even with an audible voice, Moses questioned God's leading.

I love God's response, not just what He said, but what He didn't say. He didn't build up Moses' self-confidence or self-esteem. He didn't list Moses' outstanding qualifications for the job or point out his superior training in Pharaoh's court. In fact, He basically ignored the question and simply said, "But I will be with you" (Exodus 3:12). If I may reverently rephrase

God's response: Bottom line, Moses, it doesn't matter who you are, it only matters who I am and that I will be with you.

What comfort in God's response. We, too, may face responsibilities or circumstances for which we feel inadequate. We may question our qualifications or gifts when called to a ministry. We may question God's leading for our life. God may not give us the miracle of a burning bush, but He does give us the same wonderful assurance He gave to Moses, "I will be with you!" And for me, that's better than a burning bush!

Prayer

Dear loving Father: I've always loved that one of Your names is Emmanuel, God with us. The magicians in the story of Daniel said gods don't live among men. Our God does and that truth makes all the difference. It wasn't the burning bush that gave Moses the confidence He needed; it was the assurance of Your presence. And we're promised Your presence even when there's not a burning bush. Thank You. Amen.

Stormy Winds

"He made the storm be still, and the waves
of the sea were hushed." — Psalm 107:29

This morning I was reading the account of Jesus calming the storm. If you remember the story, the disciples were facing a life-threatening storm while Jesus remained asleep and undisturbed. The disciples urged Jesus to wake up, certain they were all going to drown. Jesus simply spoke, and the wind and the raging waters became calm.

What a powerful demonstration of the authority of Jesus! The disciples were amazed and awed—even the winds obeyed the command of Jesus.

Many sermons have been preached on this text, and the point most often made is God's power to calm the storms we face in our lives. And, thankfully, He can. But there's a verse in the Psalms that adds another dimension to this truth.

Psalm 148 is a psalm of praise. In fact, the word *praise* is mentioned twelve times in the psalm's fourteen verses. But tucked among all the praise is the phrase, "stormy winds that do his bidding" (vs. 8 NIV). It's exactly what the disciples saw demonstrated in a powerful way that day on the Sea of Galilee. The stormy winds obeyed the command of the Creator and became calm.

But I believe those words also give us the assurance that God remains in control of all the stormy winds in our lives and can use them to accomplish His purposes. They all must do His bidding. Sometimes He commands them to be still, and sometimes He allows them to continue blowing. Both are under His command for His purposes. Both are doing His bidding.

I find great encouragement in that reminder on stormy days when I feel blown about by the circumstances in my life. Even the stormy winds are under His control and will be used for His purpose and His glory until the time when He says, "Be still!"

Prayer

Dear sovereign God: There is great comfort in knowing that even the winds and the waves obey You. Help us to trust You in the storm. Amen.

Steps of Surrender

"I know, O LORD, that the way of man is not in himself, that it is not in man who walks to direct steps." — Jeremiah 10:23

Not My Own

"You are not your own, for you were bought
with a price." — *1 Corinthians 6:19b,20a*

Sometimes simple, familiar phrases become new and profound. That happened to me recently as I read Paul's reminder, "You are not your own." I understand the theology of this, but the practical reality of these words really struck me. The truth that I am not my own impacts every area of my life.

If I am not my own, then I must agree with the words of Jeremiah when he declares, "I know, O Lord, that the way of man is not in himself, that it is not in man who walks to direct his steps" (Jeremiah 10:23). The One who holds ownership of me has every right to choose my steps. How wonderful to know He chooses with wisdom and is motivated by love.

If I am not my own, then to offer my body as a living sacrifice really is an act of spiritual worship. It is giving over control to the rightful owner. It also means conformity to this world can't be for me. I must instead conform to the principles and standards of an eternal kingdom (Romans 12:1,2).

If I am not my own, there is only one answer when God asks, "can I not do with you as this potter has done?" (Jeremiah 18:6). God has every right to shape me into the vessel of His choosing for His use and His glory.

And, if I am not my own, then my heart needs to echo the words of John as he declares, "He must increase, but I must decrease" (John 3:30). I must strive to allow everyone to see the wonder and glory of the One who rightfully owns me.

I must never forget the hands that reach out to claim me have scars as evidence of His right to ownership and proof of the love that makes me so thankful to say, "I am not my own!"

Prayer

Dear Father: We sometimes balk at the thought of not being our own. Help me to remember that Calvary puts this all into perspective, and I give up my rights to One who is all-wise, all-loving and will always choose best for me. Amen.

A Simple Question

"Does the clay say to him who forms it,
'What are you making?'" — Isaiah 45:9b

I have been struck by a very simple question found in Romans 9:21. "Has the potter no right over the clay?"—a simple question with profound implications. In the illustration of the potter and the clay, the answer is clear. Yes, of course. The clay simply yields to the potter's hands and becomes what the potter has chosen. In our lives, the answer is the same, but not one we always find easy to accept.

The secret to finding peace in that answer is simply in knowing and trusting the Potter. If you question the Potter's wisdom, wonder about His love, and doubt He will choose what is best, then you will find it hard to yield to His hands as they shape and form you. If you trust Him, then you will trust the work of His hands in your life.

Sometimes, it's not the end result we question, but the Potter's means of accomplishing the final vessel of His choosing. We don't like His methods. We don't like the process. Once again, the secret is in resting in the truth that His ways are not our ways. We would like to just effortlessly (and painlessly) become a beautiful vessel for His glory. But clay that won't yield to the Potter's hands (even when they seem rough) remains a useless lump of clay.

Second Corinthians 4:7 gives us a clear picture of the ultimate goal of the Potter. "But we have this treasure in jars of clay, to show that the surpassing power belongs to God and not to us." We are being formed to hold a treasure, a treasure that reveals the glory of the Potter rather than the pot.

God knows what He's doing. "Does not the potter have the right?" Absolutely! And the end result is a vessel He lovingly uses for His purposes and His glory. What more could a lump of clay ask for?

Prayer

Dear Potter: The more I know You, the easier it is to yield to Your hands as they work Your will and Your purpose in my life. May the end result be a vessel that is evidence of Your goodness for Your glory. Amen.

the end result being His work (as potter)
what is our role?
→ clay depends 100% on potter

Bloom Where You are Planted

"[T]he branch of my planting, the work of my
hands that I might be glorified." — Isaiah 60:21c

I recently saw a picture of a beautiful flower growing up through a small crack in a cement sidewalk. The caption read "bloom where you are planted." That's not a phrase you'll find in Scripture, but it is a scriptural principle.

We find an example of this in Jeremiah 29:4–7. The nation of Israel had been uprooted and taken into captivity in Babylon. God's instructions were not, "Hang in there, endure as best you can." He didn't urge them to try to muddle through until their time in Babylon was up. No, God's instructions were they were to prosper in that land—in their hard place. They were to build houses, plant gardens, and increase in number. In other words, they were to bloom where they were planted. This was not only for their best, but for His glory.

God reinforces this truth in Isaiah 60:21. Once again, referring to the nation of Israel, He says they are the work of His hands for His glory. God chose the spot and planted them there for a specific reason: to allow those around them to see His splendor.

God often places us where He can be noticed, where we can best be a display of His glory. I noticed the flower in the picture because of where it was. It wouldn't have stood out in a field full of flowers or in a beautiful garden. It stood out because of its surroundings.

We sometimes find ourselves planted in difficult places—places we wouldn't have chosen for ourselves. But God's Word to each of us is the same as it was to Israel: You are there so He can be glorified.

Underneath the cement was soil that provided the plant in the picture with all it needed to blossom. Underneath our difficult circumstances is a God who has everything we need in the hardest of places. If we put our roots down deep in Him, we can bloom wherever He has planted us for His glory!

Prayer

Dear Father: We often forget that underneath the hard circumstances we find ourselves in, there is the rich soil of Your sufficiency. Help us to "bloom where we are planted" as a beautiful display of Your glory. Amen.

That Little Word Yet

"And the world is passing away along with its desires, but whoever does the will of God abides forever." — 1 John 2:17

The scene is a garden and a lone man praying. It's a scene portrayed in great works of art and reenacted for centuries from beautiful cathedrals to small county churches. But included in the great drama of that scene is the most poignant act of surrender in all of human history. We hear the agonized cry of "My Father, if it is possible, may this cup be taken from me." But that heart wrenching plea is followed by words that are the ultimate declaration of surrender, "Yet not as I will, but as you will" (Matthew 26:39 NIV).

All of our hopes for eternity hang on that little word *yet.* In spite of the suffering, in spite of bearing an unspeakable weight of sin (our sin), in spite of the anguish of separation from the Father, Jesus uttered those amazing words of surrender to His Father's will.

That very real moment in history puts our surrender to God into perspective. He's not asking too much. He's not making an unreasonable demand. All of our excuses or fears seem meaningless in light of Jesus' choice. Our entire relationship with God is possible because of that little word *yet.* "Yet, not as

I will, but as you will" were Christ's words in Gethsemane and words that need to be echoed in our own hearts.

Surrender means we yield to the path He chooses for us. Our journey is not always an easy one. The path is not always smooth or one we would choose, but if we look at the feet of the One who walks beside us as we take big steps and little ones, we'll see scars that are an eternal reminder of His surrender for us. Surrender is simply (though not always easily) choosing that little word *yet*.

Prayer

Dear Father: There is a depth of anguish we can't fully understand that took place in Gethsemane. But there is also a depth of love that brought about the surrender of our Savior to Your will and Your purposes. It's a love that makes sense of our surrender. How dare we insist on our own way when we think of Gethsemane? May our prayer also be, "Yet not as I will, but as You will." Amen.

Those Vain Things

"But whatever gain I had, I counted as loss for the sake of Christ." — Philippians 3:7

One of the most powerful and well-loved hymns in Christendom is "When I Survey the Wondrous Cross" by Isaac Watts. It's one of the few to survive the transition from hymnbook to worship songs as it ministers to a new generation. The words of this great hymn never fail to speak to me and to make me ask myself some serious and important questions.

Recently one of those questions has come as a result of the phrase, "All the vain things that charm me most." I've been asking God to show me those things, to reveal to my heart the vain things that take my time and attention away from Him. And He's done that. My list of vain things may be different from yours, but the answer is still the same: they need to be "sacrificed to His blood." They need to be put in their proper place in our lives in light of Calvary's sacrifice.

As I get older, I sense the urgency of these days in which we live. There isn't time to waste on vain things, no matter how much they charm us. When you look up *vain* in the dictionary, you see words like worthless and useless. It's very possible Isaac Watts had in mind an older definition that implied something foolish or silly. Listen to that line again: All the worthless and useless, the foolish and silly things that hold my attention and affection, I sacrifice them to His blood.

God loves to bring joy into our lives. He loves to see us enjoying this life and doesn't expect us to spend every minute of it in church with a pious, somber attitude. But the greatest joys in this life come when we declutter and sacrifice all the vain things in order to experience those blessings and joys that come from His hand. And how can we not want to do that when we "survey the wondrous cross"?

Prayer

Dear loving Savior: It's really hard to fully comprehend all that was involved in Your death on the cross. But this I know, "Love so amazing, so divine, Demands my soul, my life, my all." May I offer those willingly to the One who offered His all for me. Amen.

David's Choice

"This God—his way is perfect." — Psalm 18:30a

The road to the throne had been a difficult one for David. He had been running and hiding for years as King Saul continually threatened his life. But finally, God's promise was fulfilled, and David was established as Israel's king. Long live the king!

Unfortunately, it wasn't long before David learned "long live the king" was not a sentiment shared by his son, and once again David was on the run. This time it was his son Absalom, his own flesh and blood, who was threatening his kingdom and his life. And it was in these circumstances David made this incredible declaration: "let him [God] do to me what seems good to him" (2 Samuel 15:26).

The context of my reading David's words made them intensely meaningful for me. I was baffled by God. Like David, my circumstances seemed to totally contradict all of God's promises. I wondered if David had struggled with any of the same emotions and questions I was experiencing?

Scripture doesn't tell us what David was feeling, but it does tell us how he responded. His words reveal a surrendered heart, even in the worst of circumstances. David saw the outcome as up to God, not up to Absalom, and he surrendered to God and to His purposes.

David's response teaches us a vitally important lesson: This was ultimately not about David and Absalom. It was about David and God. David refused to see himself at the mercy of his son, but instead recognized he was under the care of a God he trusted. David chose to yield, not to his son's evil intentions, but to a God who knew best. And that became my choice too.

Prayer

Dear loving Father: Your ways are often mysterious to us. I'm sure they were to David. But I pray our response will be like his, to yield to Your plan for us. May we echo David's words as we trust You to do to us "what seems good" to You. There is no risk in this prayer because You love us and really do know what's best. Amen.

Absolutely His

*"I will take you to be my people, and I will
be your God." — Exodus 6:7a*

Oswald Chambers once challenged a friend with these
words: "Be absolutely His!" Imagine what our lives
would be like if we truly were absolutely His. I looked up the
word *absolutely*, and each definition adds so much more emphasis to that thought. Be unconditionally, wholly, positively,
completely, unquestionably, and totally His. Those words im-
ply no compromise, no half-hearted giving over. They make it
clear there are no exceptions or conditions.

This may seem like a risky choice. What a difference it
makes when we know the One to whom we are yielding. We
are given every assurance in Scripture that He loves us with a
love that can't be measured. We're assured of His vast wisdom
coupled with His great power. We know He has complete
authority now and forever. What a privilege to give ourselves
completely to such an amazing and wonderful God—to be
absolutely His.

But what's even more amazing is God is willing to be absolutely ours. Over and over in Scripture He says, "and I will be
their God." He continually worked to restore relationship with

His people, Israel, so He could be their God. He went to the extreme of Calvary so He could be our God. But the best news of all is this is His eternal goal. In Revelation 21:3b it says: "They will be his people, and God himself will be with them as their God." God Himself will be unconditionally, wholly, positively, definitely, completely, unquestionably, and totally ours forever and ever. And won't that be absolutely wonderful!

Prayer

Dear loving God: There is something in us that wants to hold back from total surrender. It feels risky. We want to maintain some control, to have some say in our lives. But the more we know You, the more we know there can be no wiser or safer choice for us than to be absolutely, unconditionally Yours. May this be a reality in our lives. Amen.

Prayerful Steps

"The prayer of a righteous person has great power as it is working." — James 5:16b

Faith vs. Facts

"The Lord is faithful in all his words, and
kind in all his works." — Psalm 145:13b

What happens when your faith and the facts contradict each other? That's what Abraham faced. He was about one-hundred years old and Sarah's biological clock had stopped ticking long ago, and they had no children. Those were the facts! But God had made a promise to Abraham—a promise that Abraham would become the father of many nations. I love what Scripture tells us about Abraham as he faced the faith vs. facts dilemma. He didn't ignore the facts or pretend they weren't true; they simply didn't impact his faith.

Abraham's faith could look at the facts with a confidence they wouldn't keep God from fulfilling His promise. God's promise trumped the harsh reality of facts. Romans 4:20 puts it like this: "No unbelief made him waver concerning the promise of God."

I'm facing a similar situation. The facts look dismal and discouraging, but I have a promise God has given me in His Word, and I will cling to His promise despite the facts. God's Word is the basis for my faith—not the facts of the situation.

The end of my story hasn't been written yet, but we know the end of Abraham's story. All God promised became a reality. "Against all hope, Abraham in hope believed and so became the father of many nations, *just as it had been said to him*" (Romans 4:18 NIV emphasis added).

Are you struggling with facts vs. faith? Remember the example of Abraham who "did not weaken in faith" and even though he faced the facts that he was old and Sarah was barren, he was "fully convinced that God was able to do what he had promised" (Romans 4:21). Whatever the facts of your situation, remember faith rests in the greatest fact of all—God is faithful to His Word and His promises.

Prayer

Dear faithful Father: The facts often are contrary to Your promises. They certainly were for Abraham. Give us the faith to look past the facts and rest in Your promises. May Your Word be the foundation of our faith. Amen.

Context Makes All
the Difference

"[C]asting all your anxieties on him,
because he cares for you." — 1 Peter 5:7

There are Christian phrases that become so familiar we can easily miss the added depth that comes from reading them in context. One of those phrases, and one I've been working at applying to my own life in recent days, is "do not be anxious about anything" (Philippians 4:6). Those words are quite a challenge, especially when there are real circumstances and concerns that seem like pretty valid reasons to be anxious.

Paul was not sending the church in Philippi a slogan, words to be hung on the wall or sewn on a pillow. Those words were never meant to stand alone. "Do not be anxious about anything" is tucked between two truths that give us solid reasons to live without anxiety.

The words immediately preceding Paul's call to live without being anxious are, "The Lord is at hand." It's not just that the Lord sees or is aware of our situation, but He Himself is near. God stands by us as "a very present help" in our times of trouble (Psalm 46:1). The more we know the Lord, the more we will find His presence a perfect antidote for anxiety. But that's not all. The words "do not be anxious about anything" are not only preceded by the assurance of God's presence, they're followed by words instructing us how to deal with our anxiety. Paul reminds us there's something we can do in situations where it seems like there's nothing we can do. We can pray.

"Do not be anxious about anything" is a tall order. These words taken by themselves can be hard to achieve when life seems to offer us legitimate reasons for anxiety. But take those same words and tuck them between the wonderful assurance of God's presence and our freedom to unburden our hearts to Him in prayer, and we find solid ground for our feet to stand, anxious-free, during difficult days.

Prayer

Dear loving Father: I can't imagine life without prayer, without being able to bring all the things that are cause for anxiety to You. Thank You for the assurance that in our anxious times You are near. And thank You for the amazing privilege of casting all those anxieties on You in prayer with the assurance we can because You care for us. Amen.

Ask Big!

"Is anything too hard for the LORD?" — *Genesis 18:14a*

Recently I watched an episode of a program called *House Crashers*. The host, Josh, roams through a home improvement store in search of someone who needs work done somewhere in their house. Josh then offers to come home with them, look at their house, and fix whatever needs to be done in at least one room—all for free! Not a bad deal. He then asks what they would like done, what changes they'd like to see. But what really struck me was when he was asking one couple what they would like to see done, he said this, "Ask big! Ask big!" Why not? Someone else was paying so why not ask big? How silly it would be to ask to have the counters cleaned or to have a light bulb changed when someone offered to provide all that was needed to completely makeover the room exactly how you wanted it to be.

Ask big! We have a God who offers us that same challenge. We have a God who declares He can do "far more abundantly than all that we ask or think, according to the power at work within us" (Ephesians 3:20). We have a God who challenged Jeremiah to call on Him, with the assurance He would show him great and mighty things beyond Jeremiah's knowledge

(Jeremiah 33:3). We have a God who declares there is absolutely nothing too hard for Him. So why not "ask big" because we have a God who can answer big.

We see a wonderful example of this in the life of Moses. After asking for the promise of God's presence, he then asked, "Now show me Your glory!" (Exodus 33:18 NIV). Moses dared to ask big and was not disappointed.

Do you have big needs? Ask big. We have a God who loves to give big answers!

Prayer

Dear Almighty God: How silly to ask puny prayers of a great God. I think of the warning in James that we don't have simply because we don't ask. Help us to trust You to give big answers to our big needs because You are a big God. Amen.

The Battle Behind the Battle

*"Who is this King of glory? The Lord strong and
mighty, the Lord, mighty in battle!" — Psalm 24:8*

The story of Israel's battle over the Amalekites is one of my
favorites. We see two scenes being played out at the same
time. One is Joshua and the army of Israel with their swords
and shields engaged in the harsh reality of battle. The other
is Moses standing on a hilltop overlooking the battle with
the staff of God in his hands raised toward heaven. He didn't
have a sword drawn. He wasn't face-to-face with an Amale-
kite, but his position was crucial to the outcome of this battle. Exodus 17:11 states, "Whenever Moses held up his hand,
Israel prevailed, and whenever he lowered his hand, Amalek
prevailed."

Even with so much at stake, Moses' hands became tired. (I
don't know if you've ever tried to hold your hands up for any
length of time, but it becomes very exhausting.) Thankfully,
Aaron and Hur stepped in and supported the weary arms of
Moses, and Israel was victorious.

When the battle was over, we find God gives Moses some
interesting instructions. Moses was told to write down the
events so they would always be remembered, but God specifi-

cally told Moses to make sure Joshua heard about it. Why did God make a point of saying Joshua needed to hear this?

Joshua was the one out there in the sweat and blood of battle, but I believe God wanted him to know prayer was the real weapon, and God was the real victor. The reason for the victory was hands lifted up to the throne of God.

What an important lesson for us today. We're in a battle, and the good news is the outcome doesn't depend on our skill. Hands lifted up to the throne of God are still the key to victory!

Prayer

Dear mighty God: I'm thankful You instructed Moses to write down these events. I think we need to be reminded of this as much as Joshua did. The war was fought on the battlefield, but the victory was won on the hillside. Help us to never try to fight without hands lifted to You. That's our only hope of victory. Amen.

The Unseen God

"Though you have not seen him, you love him." — 1 Peter 1:8a

Do you ever find it difficult to pray to an unseen God? I have. I remember many times when I would say, "I just wish You could come and sit beside me so I could talk to you face-to-face." One day I was trying so hard during my prayer time to *sense* God. I found myself trying to imagine Him, to conjure up some image or expression of Him to make it easier to talk to Him and to share my heart.

God used a young friend of mine to teach me a precious lesson that day. I've known Britni since she was a baby. In fact, I have the privilege of being her Aunt Esther even though we're not really related. I've watched her grow up, but Britni has never seen me. She was born blind.

It's amazing to me how Britni immediately knows when I'm there. Even as a very little girl she recognized my voice and would very confidently start talking to me when I came into the room. She didn't have to see me. She didn't have to try to imagine me or to conjure up some image in her mind to make it possible for her to talk to me. She just knew I was there. She knew my voice and would simply begin to share whatever was on her heart. It never occurred to Britni to doubt the reality of my presence. She was confident I was there and was just as confident I was listening to whatever she had to say.

What a wonderful reminder. I can't see God, but it doesn't make His presence any less real. I, too, have learned to know His voice, and can share whatever is on my heart with Him, confident He's there, and confident He's listening.

Thank you, Britni. Thank you for being used of God to teach your Aunt Esther a wonderful lesson.

Prayer

Dear omnipresent God: We look forward so much to the day when we will see you face-to-face. What an amazing day it will truly be. But until that day, help us to take You at Your word. You are with us, always present, always ready to listen. Thank You for this wonderful assurance. Amen.

In Jesus' Name, Amen

"Some trust in chariots and some in horses, but we trust in the name of the LORD our God." — Psalm 20:7

Years before the birth of Christ, Isaiah announced the names that would be given to Mary's child, the Messiah. "And his name shall be called Wonderful Counselor, Mighty God, Everlasting Father, Prince of Peace" (Isaiah 9:6c). Have you ever thought of the significance of those names when you pray?

How often do we come to the Lord when we need His insight and wisdom? When we pray in Jesus' name, we're praying in the name of the Wonderful Counselor, the all-wise God. We're praying to One who knows us, who knows our needs, who knows the problems we face. There's nothing beyond the wisdom and help of this Wonderful Counselor!

Jesus was also given the name Mighty God, the all-powerful One. We pray to One who through the power of His words spoke this amazing world into existence. One who held back the waters of the Red Sea, who shut the mouths of lions, who brought Lazarus out of the tomb. There is simply no need we bring to Him in prayer for which His power isn't adequate.

And to pray "in Jesus' name" also means we pray to an eternal Father. I had a wonderful father so it's easy for me to pray with assurance that the One who hears loves me and will protect and provide—all the things a good father does. But how wonderful for those who didn't have a father, or didn't have a good father, to come with their needs to a perfect Father.

In John 14:27c, Jesus tells His disciples, "Let not your hearts be troubled, neither let them be afraid." That seems like a lot to ask, except He has just promised them that when He returns to His Father, He will leave His peace with them. He reminds them His peace is different from the world's peace. How wonderful to know in times of stress or worry Jesus offers us His peace, a peace truly beyond our understanding.

The names of Jesus cover every need we may have. No wonder the psalmist said, "And those who know Your name put their trust in you" (Psalm 9:10).

Prayer

Dear sufficient God: I love Your names! I love how they remind us You truly are sufficient for each and every need we may have. Your names make that very clear. What a privilege it is to pray in Jesus' name(s). Amen.

Teach Me to Pray

"[T]he prayer of the upright is acceptable
to him." — Proverbs 15:8b

Jesus often left His disciples and went to a quiet place to pray. It was after one of these times one of His disciples asked, "Lord, teach us to pray" (Luke 11:1). Have you ever noticed how Christ responded to his disciples after their request? He prayed! He prayed a prayer commonly referred to as the Lord's Prayer, possibly the most famous and well-known prayer of all times.

There have been many sermons preached on the Lord's Prayer, and it's been the subject of many books. It has been studied phrase by phrase and dissected into parts considered the elements of a good prayer. While none of this is wrong, I think the real lesson Jesus taught that day is often missed. In response to their request, Christ didn't give them a lecture on prayer. He didn't analyze the different aspects of prayer or talk to them about faith. He simply prayed! Perhaps this was the real lesson. He demonstrated this simple truth to His disciples. If you want to learn to pray, then pray!

After all, if you want to learn to cook, you don't just read cookbooks. You cook. If you want to learn to swim, you don't just watch videos on the various swimming strokes; you get into the water. And, if you want to learn to pray, you should pray! There is no greater teacher than experience.

I remember going through a time when I was determined to become more faithful in my prayer life. Soon my bookshelf was full of books on prayer, good books on prayer, helpful books on prayer. But my prayer life didn't change until I stopped reading about prayer and began to pray.

Is your heart longing to ask the same request of Christ? "Lord, teach me to pray." Learn from His response to His disciples and simply begin praying!

Prayer

Dear Father: Praying is one of the most amazing privileges, but it's also one of our greatest needs. Jesus left us so much more than the words of the Lord's Prayer. He left us a powerful example by His own life of prayer. May we follow His example and pray! Amen.

Steps Led by Love

"Your steadfast love, O Lord, extends to the heavens." — Psalm 36:5a

The Adventure of Loving God

*"May the Lord direct your hearts
to the love of God." — 2 Thessalonians 3:5a*

In the book *A Harvest of Yesteryears*, Gladys Tabor says this, "Loving is, after all, an adventure into another personality." In other words, love takes the focus off ourselves and instead explores the heart and character of the one we love.

Jesus made it clear that the first and greatest commandment is we love God, not just with emotional warmth, but with a passion involving all of our heart and mind and strength. We are to pour our whole being into the adventure of God's great personality.

I've been married for quite a few years, and I'm still finding new depths to my husband. That's one of the joys of marriage. I have friends who continue to surprise me with new aspects of their personalities.

But what is true on the human level is true to a much greater degree with God. There is no end to loving God. There is no end to this great adventure of exploring the heights and depths of His nature. God can be known, but He can never be fully known, which means this adventure of love will never end.

Scripture makes this very clear when it reminds us knowing God is what heaven is all about. John 17:3 defines eternal life as an eternal opportunity to know God. Listen to these words: "And this is eternal life, that they may know you, the only true God, and Jesus Christ, whom you have sent." This is eternal life, the continual adventure into the personality and nature of our God. We'll have all of eternity to know and love Him.

There may be no end to knowing and loving God, but there is a beginning. We don't have to wait until heaven. An old song by the Teddy Bears declared, "To know, know, know him is to love, love, love him." I don't know how true it was of the boy they were singing about, but I do know how wonderfully true it is of God.

Prayer

Dear infinite God: There is no end to knowing You. Forgive us for sometimes seeing this as an impersonal relationship or a religion when You have intended it to always be a love relationship. To know You is to love You, and to love You is to want to know You more—truly a glorious adventure. Amen.

A Steadfast Love

"[C]onsider the steadfast love of the LORD." — Psalm 107:43b

Do you realize how often the words *steadfast* and *love* are linked together in Scripture? I'm sure there's a website where I could find the exact number of times, but the exact number isn't important—it's the emphasis God brings to this truth through His repeated use of that phrase.

Proverbs 19:22 reminds us "What is desired in a man is steadfast love." I think most of us would agree, especially if at some point we've experienced the failure of human love.

The wonderful news is God offers us a love that comes with a guarantee. It won't stop or diminish; it won't disappear just when we need it the most. His love will never fail to watch over us, to care for us. It will never fail to comfort, protect, and sometimes discipline us.

God's steadfast love is a love that brings blessings, yet permits sorrow. It's a love that will never fail to choose which of those is best and perfect for us. But above all else, it's a love that became "obedient to the point of death, even death on a cross" (Philippians 2:8)! There is simply no other explanation for Calvary apart from the steadfast, unfailing love of God. The hymn writer reminds us even if there was a whole ocean full of ink, it wouldn't be enough to adequately express the love of God. But there was a man on a cross who remains a powerful and dramatic display of that love. If it were possible for God's love to fail, it would have failed then.

God's love isn't just deep, it isn't just forever—it's steadfast. Human love can increase or diminish. Human love can be selfish and self-serving. But God's love is forever the same.

Do you need to experience steadfast love? I would encourage you to consider the great unwavering love of God.

Prayer

Dear loving Father: I find myself at a loss for words to fully express the wonder of Your love. It is an illogical love. We aren't always lovable, and yet You always love. We can do nothing to earn Your love, and yet You offer it freely. And best of all, it is steadfast and will never fail. Thank You that Your love comes with a guarantee. Amen.

God is Never Indifferent

*"[W]hat is man that you are mindful of him, and the
son of man that you care for him?" — Psalm 8:4*

Aunt Hazel was a gruff but lovable old lady. She heard
somewhere it was a good thing to talk to your plants, so
she decided to try it. She reported to us later that after planting
some flowers in her yard, she got up, looked down at them,
and said, "Live or die. It don't make any difference to me!" and
walked away. We had a good laugh at Aunt Hazel's conversation with her plants, but what she conveyed by those remarks
was she really didn't care about them one way or the other. She
had planted them but was indifferent to their outcome.

Do you know God is never indifferent? There's not one in-
stance in Scripture where we see God being ambivalent toward
those He created. In fact, we see many examples that reveal just
the opposite. In Genesis 6:6 it says when God saw the sinfulness
of man, His heart was grieved. Can you imagine that? The heart
of God experienced deep sadness because of man's sin.

We also read of times when God's heart overflows with delight and joy in His children. I love the verse that declares God
takes great delight in us and even rejoices over us with singing
(Zephaniah 3:17). God is deeply vested in us emotionally. He

cares, He can be grieved, and He can experience great joy, but He is never indifferent. We matter to Him.

Aunt Hazel's plants really didn't matter to her. Her brief conversation with them clearly conveyed that message. God is not like Aunt Hazel. He does care—deeply. I don't know about you, but I don't ever want to bring pain to the heart of God. I want to live in a way that brings Him great joy, maybe even so much I'll hear Him sing.

Prayer

Dear loving God: It is an amazing and wonderful truth that You care deeply about us. There's no human comparison to Your depth of care and concern. And the only explanation for that is Your great love. I imagine there are times when we aren't much more lovable than Aunt Hazel's plants, and yet it matters to You whether or not we grow and bloom. You are a good God and You care. Amen.

The Right Kind of Jealousy

"And you shall be my people, and I will be your God." — Jeremiah 30:22

Have you ever felt jealous? Jealousy is usually considered a negative trait, yet most of us have experienced that feeling at one time or another. We see someone get a promotion we thought we deserved, or a friend gets a new home or a car we can't afford and we feel jealous. Sometimes jealousy rears up when we see someone thinner, or younger, or smarter and begin to feel the stirrings of what has been called the "green-eyed monster."

But then we read in Scripture God is a jealous God. As a child I found those words a little disturbing. It seemed like something that shouldn't be part of God's nature. After all, jealousy's not a good thing—or is it?

One of the first things God declared to His people Israel was He alone was to be their God. Israel was not to worship any other god but Him, and God declares it's because He is a jealous God (Exodus 20:5). But God's jealousy doesn't come from "green eyes," it comes instead from a loving heart. His jealousy is not rooted in envy or greed, but rather stems from a desire to watch over and protect His children for their sake. It's the jealousy a mother has over her children.

God is still a jealous God. He still insists on being the only object of our worship. He still guards our affection with a pure and right jealousy, a jealousy always for our good to protect and guard us. It's never based on envy or selfishness, but always from the purest motive—love.

It's really a wonderful thing to have a jealous God, a God who insists we be His alone and our love and worship be for Him alone. We are so blessed to have a God with the perfect kind of jealousy.

Prayer

Dear heavenly Father: Your Father's heart is the reason for Your jealousy. It's part of Your deep love for us that desires only what is best. And You are what is best! Help us to keep our hearts for You alone. Amen.

Spiritual Stretching

*"See what great love the Father
has lavished on us." —1 John 3:1a (NIV)*

God has been stretching me. He's been stretching my mind to take in greater thoughts about who He is and stretching my heart to receive greater depths of His love. Something I've learned as He's been stretching me is that the more I understand His greatness—His absolute holiness, His infinite wisdom, His sovereignty and power—the more I am overwhelmed by His love.

I realize Calvary stands as the ultimate demonstration of God's love, but I believe the words in John 17:23 are the ultimate declaration of that love. These words are taken from one of the last recorded prayers of Jesus. As He's praying for Himself, for His disciples, and for all believers, Jesus utters these amazing words: "so that the world may know that you sent me and loved them even as you loved me." Imagine! This amazing and glorious God loves us as much as He loves His own perfect Son. You read that right. It is a stunningly profound comment and truth.

I understand the love of the Father for His Son. What's not to love? But I can't understand the same love ("even as" the Scripture assures us) being directed toward me. What's to love? And yet, that's really what true love is all about, what God's love is all about. It's not based on the recipient's worth, but on the heart of the One who loves.

I'm not a big fan of physical exercise. I don't deny its value; I'm just not a big fan. But having my mind and heart stretched by God is the best exercise there is. God, who is infinitely above the sum total of my thoughts about Him (even when my mind has been stretched), loves me and is stretching my heart to receive more and more of His love. The hymnist says it best: "Amazing love! how can it be? That Thou my God shouldst die for me." Just try to stretch your mind around that!

Prayer

Dear God: It really is hard to grasp the extent and depth of Your love. It's amazing that You love us, but Paul is right when he says this love truly surpasses knowledge. The only response to Your love is to bow humbly before You with a heart filled with worship and love. Thank You for loving me. Amen.

A Good Enough Reason

"The Lord is good...He cares for those
who trust in him." — Nahum 1:7 (NIV)

A frequently quoted verse is 1 Peter 5:7: "casting all your anxieties on him, because he cares for you." I know there are times when our anxiety seems more than we can bear, and it's hard to put these words into practice. We're worried about our health or the health of someone we love. Maybe our finances keep us awake at night, or one of our children is causing us a great deal of worry. Whatever the specific anxiety may be, it comes under the "all" of 1 Peter 5:7. There are no exceptions. We're to cast *all* of our anxiety on Him.

I believe there's a strong correlation between the first and the last part of that verse. I suspect our ability to free ourselves of our anxieties—to cast them on the Lord—deeply depends on how much we believe the second part of the verse. "Casting all your anxiety on Him *because* He cares for you" (emphasis added). The absolute truth is God really does care for us, not in a generic sense, but in the deepest, most personal sense of the word. He cares! He cares about our health, He cares about our finances, and He cares about the child causing us heartache. The more we realize the truth of those words, the easier it becomes to cast all our anxieties on Him.

God cares for us. He's demonstrated the extent of His love and care on a cross. And because of His care, He asks us—urges us—to bring everything to Him that's causing us to worry, to lose sleep, or to be afraid.

God's invitation to cast all our cares on Him is deeply rooted in the wonderful truth that He cares for us, and it seems to me that's a good enough reason.

Prayer

Dear loving God: We often have legitimate reasons to be anxious. There are very real problems or concerns. Help us to remember there is also a very real God who truly cares about us. May that give us the courage and confidence to cast all our cares on You no matter how justified our anxieties may seem. We can trust You to care for all that concerns us. Amen.

Guaranteed Maintenance

*"God who keeps his covenant and steadfast love
with those who love him."* — *Nehemiah 1:5b*

I love the endless discoveries found in God's Word. This morning I was reading a familiar passage in Exodus where God reveals His nature to Moses. He's already declared Himself to Moses as the great "I AM"—a description of God that I love. But then He shares more of His nature as He proclaims He is "The LORD, the LORD, the compassionate and gracious God, slow to anger, abounding in love and faithfulness, maintaining love to thousands, and forgiving wickedness, rebellion and sin" Exodus 34:6–7a (NIV).

What a powerful description of the Almighty. But the phrase that caught my attention this morning as I read those words was one I hadn't particularly noticed before. God says He is "maintaining love to thousands." I looked up maintain in the dictionary and found this definition: "to preserve from failure or decline." God maintains His love for us. He preserves it. He keeps it from failure or decline. It will never end and it will never diminish.

We continually get phone calls from people trying to sell us an extended warranty on our car. That's because they know promises from dealerships to maintain a car are limited. They simply don't promise to maintain a car indefinitely. No one would expect them to.

But God's guarantee has no expiration date. He has promised to maintain His love. No wonder the hymn writer wrote, "O, love of God, how rich and pure! How measureless and strong! It shall forevermore endure." God's love will last forever! Isn't that a glorious truth? "It shall forevermore endure" because God has promised He will maintain it. He will preserve it and keep it from failure or decline.

Maybe you've experienced the failure or disappointment of human love—love you thought would last forever. What assurance we have from God's own words. His love for us will never fail because it's being maintained by Him. Now that's a wonderful guarantee!

Prayer

Dear unfailing God: I think the hymn writer must have realized the certainty of Your love when he wrote: "O love that will not let me go." We are so grateful for the guarantee of that kind of love. Thank You for maintaining Your love for us so it will last throughout all of eternity. Amen.

Daily Steps

"So teach us to number our days that we may get a heart of wisdom." — Psalm 90:12

What Are We Here For?

"So, whether you eat or drink, or whatever you do,
do all to the glory of God." — 1 Corinthians 10:31

Often, when we walk through the doors of our grocery store, my husband will ask, "What are we here for?" That's actually a good question to ask before we begin shopping. It determines if we should get a big cart or a little basket. It also gives us a sense of direction. Should we head to the freezer section for ice cream or to the produce department for some fresh vegetables?

If we don't know why we're there, we often just wander the aisles—wandering that usually ends at the snack aisle. Often, we spend more than we intended, come home with items we really didn't need, and forget some we did need.

The early church fathers also understood the importance of that question, not for the grocery store, but for life. The first question of the Westminster Catechism asks, "What is the chief end of man?" In other words, it's the same question my husband asks as we enter the grocery store. "What are we here for?" Without the right answer, we can often wander aimlessly through life and come away with the wrong things.

The conclusion of our forefathers is an echo of Scripture—we are here to glorify God and to enjoy Him forever. Knowing this gives us purpose and direction for our lives. It influences our choices, our priorities, and our focus.

David found this purpose for his life. The Psalms are filled with words proclaiming God's glory, and we hear David's heart as he declares: "You make known to me the path of life; in your presence there is fullness of joy" (Psalm 16:11).

The question "what are we here for?" is important in the grocery store, but so much more important for our lives. We find direction (what aisles we need to be in) when we understand our purpose is to glorify God and enjoy Him forever.

Prayer

Dear Father: It helps us so much to be aware of why we're here. Help us to fulfill Your purpose for our lives as we seek to bring You glory and to find joy in our relationship with You, now and forever. Amen.

Magnificent Wisdom
for the Mundane

"I will instruct you and teach you in the
way you should go." — Psalm 32:8a

We tend to delegate God's instructions and wisdom to the spiritual areas of our lives. Thankfully, God doesn't make that distinction. In Isaiah 28:26 we read, "For he is rightly instructed; his God teaches him." And then verse 29 goes on to declare: "This also comes from the LORD of hosts; he is wonderful in counsel and excellent in wisdom."

And who is this for? Who is the beneficiary of this magnificent wisdom? Is this offer for someone facing a powerful ministry opportunity, for a prophet or priest? No, the recipient of this wisdom is the farmer. God's instructions are about plowing and planting, reaping and threshing.

I love the story of the kings on their way to battle who found themselves in the desert with no water for themselves or their horses. They asked the prophet Elisha to pray for them. I imagine they were surprised by God's response. God instructed them to dig ditches. They may have been prepared to fast and pray or to spend time worshipping, but God gave them some very practical wisdom. Dig ditches! And the next morning, the ditches were filled with water. As they obeyed and did their rather mundane part, God did His miraculous part.

Jesus told some discouraged fishermen where to put down their nets. They had been putting down their nets most of the night, and they may have rolled their eyes at His suggestion. But they did what they could (put down their nets), and God did what they couldn't and filled them with fish.

I find that so encouraging. God cares about our daily routine, our mundane work and responsibilities. The most ordinary things we face in a day are opportunities for God to instruct us and teach us the right way, and to offer us His wonderful counsel and excellent wisdom. If He's willing to instruct a man planting seeds, three kings in a desert, or discouraged fishermen, I believe He's willing to do the same for any situation we may face no matter how ordinary, and I find that wonderful news!

Prayer

Dear sovereign God: Sometimes we do You the disservice of assuming You only care about the spiritual things in our lives. I am so grateful You are an intensely practical God who is willing to give us Your wisdom, even for the mundane. Thank You! Amen.

From Information to Application

"For the word of God is living and active." — *Hebrews 4:12a*

Recently I was listening to a news program as they were discussing an important current issue. There was a great deal of information being passed back and forth—a lot of passionate concern about the issue at hand. But finally, one newsman simply asked, "But what do I do with this information?" All the information being discussed was meaningless until he could find out how it impacted his own life personally. Discussing the issue alone had no impact. The importance was found in one man's question. What difference does this make in my life? What do I need to do in response to this information?

God asks us to be just like the newsman. He's given us His Word—full of information, full of wisdom, and guiding principles—but He asks us not just to read it or discuss it, but to find out how to make His words meaningful in our own lives, how to make His words practical and applicable. In fact, God warns that to just be aware of His words and to not act on them is to deceive ourselves. He challenges us not to be simply hearers (or readers) of His Word, but to be doers—to apply what we read and hear to our daily lives (James 1:22–25).

I imagine all of that team of news people left the broadcast feeling they were more informed, more up to date on that particular issue. But unless they responded like their colleague and asked themselves the all-important question, "What do I do with this information?" they had deceived themselves.

I pray as we read God's Word, we will have the heart of that newsman and ask, "What do I do in my life with what God says?" God really does intend for His Word to be that lamp for our feet and the light for our path (Psalm 119:105) on our journey with Him.

Prayer

Dear Father: We sometimes tend to separate the spiritual from the dailiness of our lives. You never intended there to be separation. Your Word was meant to be practical and to offer us wisdom for our journey through life. Help us to learn to apply what we read to our daily steps. Amen.

It's Okay to Be Ordinary

*"God chose what is low and despised in the world...
so that no human being might boast in the
presence of God." — 1 Corinthians 1:28–29*

I have a quote in the front of my Bible by Oswald Chambers: "It is ingrained in us that we have to do exceptional things for God—but we do not. We have to be exceptional in the ordinary things of life, and holy on the ordinary streets, among ordinary people."

Do you ever struggle with feeling ordinary? Let me encourage you with a wonderful reminder: God loves to use the ordinary.

The Christmas story is about an extraordinary event, but one of the things I find encouraging each time I read it is God's use of the ordinary. Joseph was a carpenter and Mary a simple young girl, but they were God's choice as parents for His only son. An ordinary feeding trough was the first bed for the Son of God. And it was to ordinary shepherds the angels first announced the amazing news that God had come to Earth.

The feeding of the five thousand is a dramatic and amazing story. But one of the main characters of this drama was an ordinary boy with a very ordinary bag lunch. It's what Jesus did with an ordinary lunch that became extraordinary.

God chose ordinary fishermen to be His companions. But these common fishermen changed the world. Acts 4:13 says the Jewish leaders "perceived that they were uneducated, common men, they were astonished. And they recognized that they had been with Jesus."

I love the reminder in 2 Corinthians 4:7: "But we have this treasure in jars of clay, to show that the surpassing power belongs to God and not to us." What a privilege to be an ordinary clay jar because ordinary is the best backdrop for His glory!

Prayer

Dear Father: Sometimes we confuse ordinary with insignificant. The Scripture is full of incidents that contradict that. Grant us the wonderful privilege of being an ordinary clay jar for Your glory. Amen.

Who Are You?

"I can do all things through him who
strengthens me." — Philippians 4:13

Do you know who you are? It may sound like an odd question, but if someone had asked Gideon that question, he would have immediately responded, "Yes, I know who I am. I am the least in my family and part of the weakest clan in the little half tribe of Manasseh." Actually, that's exactly how he did describe himself to God in Judges 6:15. The least of the weakest is not a very powerful endorsement.

And yet, listen to how the angel of the Lord addressed him. He said, "The LORD is with you, O mighty man of valor" (Judges 6:12). Mighty man of valor? Nothing about Gideon qualified him for that title. In fact, at the time of the angel's visit, Gideon was secretly threshing grain in a winepress, hiding from the Midianites. Not the fearless act you would imagine of a "man of valor."

But God was describing Gideon as He saw him—as the man he would become. What was the difference between Gideon's view of himself and God's view of Gideon? It's found in these five simple words: The Lord is with you (Judges 6:16). Gideon was right in his evaluation of himself. He wasn't feeling sorry for himself or struggling with an inferiority complex. He had a pretty good understanding of who he was. But God knew His presence could transform even the least of the weakest into a mighty warrior.

Do you know who you are? Whatever your answer to that question may be, never forget that God's presence can transform you from what you are to what He has called you to be. He can transform a life controlled by fear, to a life of boldness that comes from the assurance of God's presence. He did it for Gideon and He can do it for you.

Prayer

Dear mighty God: What a powerful demonstration we see in the life of Gideon. It wasn't because he determined to make something of himself, but simply because the assurance that Your calling on his life came with the promise of Your presence. It still does for us today! Thank You that this is more than an Old Testament story but a present-day truth. Amen.

Duty or Love

"[F]or God loves a cheerful giver." — 2 Corinthians 9:7b

The Song of Solomon chronicles the love relationship between Solomon and his beloved. It's a beautiful picture of human love but also considered by most Bible scholars to be a picture of Christ's love for us, His beloved. However, it's near the end of the book where we find a clear picture of the distinction between duty and love.

Solomon's beloved shares the fact that Solomon owns a vineyard in Baal Hamon, which he rents out to tenants. This is strictly a business deal between Solomon and his tenants. The tenants are given the use of the vineyard and in response they are obligated to pay Solomon 1,000 shekels from their profits.

Then Solomon's beloved declares she too has a vineyard. The difference is, it is her vineyard, and she makes it clear it's hers to do with as she pleases. Yet, from her profits she offers Solomon 1,000 shekels. It is not her duty, but her choice.

In each case Solomon receives 1,000 shekels, but there was a difference in the heart and motive behind the giving. One is motivated by a business deal—a sense of duty—the other purely by love. I imagine the beloved's 1,000 shekels brought great joy to Solomon's heart.

This incident poses an interesting question. Do we give to the Lord (whether time or money or worship) out of a sense of duty or from a heart of love? It's not what we give to the Lord, but the motive behind our giving. Do we see ourselves as God's tenants, responsible to give Him only what we owe, or do we gladly offer Him what is ours out of a heart of pure love? The offering is often the same, but the heart behind the offering is what pleases God. I think it must bring Him great joy when we give Him our 1,000 shekels just because we love Him.

Prayer

Dear heavenly Father: Forgive us for the times we give to You out of a sense of duty or obligation. You have given us so much, so freely. We live surrounded by Your blessings. Help us to take what we feel is ours and offer it to You with outstretched hands of love. Amen.

Digging for Gold

"Let the word of Christ dwell in you richly." — Colossians 3:16a

I've never watched a full episode of the reality show about the men who look for gold, but I've seen enough from the short clips advertising it to know one thing for certain: finding gold is the passion of these men. There isn't much they won't do in their quest to find gold. They are willing to jeopardize life and limb for the sake of gold. Finding gold has become their priority, and it impacts every area of their lives.

David declares in Psalm 19 that the Word of God is even more precious than gold, and to make sure we really understand the value he places on it, he adds that God's Word is even of greater worth than much fine gold (Psalm 19:10). He's not comparing God's Word to a little nugget or some impure gold. He compares it to a rich supply of pure and priceless gold.

David reminds us God's Word gives light to the eyes and joy to the heart, and it's right and trustworthy, perfect and sure. In another psalm, David shares it's a lamp that allows him to see his next step, and a light for his path ahead (Psalm 119:105).

David was passionate about the Word of God. Just as the men on those reality shows have made the search for gold their priority, David made God's Word his priority. I doubt he allowed many things to stand in the way of digging into Scripture to find the nuggets of truth that could be found there.

There's no doubt gold is of great value. But there was no doubt in David's heart and mind that the Word of God was of even greater value. Maybe it's time for us to get passionate about gold—the pure gold of Scripture—and to make it a priority that will impact every area of our walk with God. After all, it's of greater worth than even much fine gold.

Prayer

Dear Holy God: David wasn't just making a nice analogy. He was stating a truth about the value of Your Word. We live in a day and age with such easy access to it that sometimes I fear we take it for granted. Help us to value Your Word. Help us to become passionate in our search for the truth found within its pages and to treat it as it should be treated—as precious as pure gold. Amen.

Help for the Journey

The Lord is my helper; I will not fear. — Hebrews 13:6b

Better Than Our Best

*"I can do all things through him who
strengthens me." — Philippians 4:13*

There's someone I know who is struggling with some serious issues. He is truly using all of his willpower and determination to deal with these, only to experience repeated defeat. He has really good intentions, but they have yet to lead to success. His is a valiant but unproductive effort.

I was struck this morning by the scriptural answer to his problem. Zechariah 4:6 reminds us it's "Not by might, nor by power, but by my Spirit." God offers a better solution for our struggles, one that doesn't depend on our own strength, but simply on our choice to yield to His Spirit. It depends on our willingness to give up and get out of the way so God can do what only God can do through His Spirit. And then, just in case we have any doubts about the validity of these words, we are reminded the One speaking is the Lord Almighty, the One with unlimited power. Ephesians 1:19 assures us of the "immeasurable greatness of his power toward us who believe." What an amazing assurance!

The context of the words in Zechariah 4:6 adds another dimension of hope. They are God's assurance of success to

Zerubbabel. Zerubbabel was facing the daunting task of rebuilding the temple. I'm sure he felt less than capable for this job. Like Zerubbabel, and like my friend, we may find our best efforts are not enough, but the work of God's Spirit brings the confidence of victory.

Are you struggling with something in your life? Are you tired of trying and failing—of giving it your best effort only to experience defeat, again? God offers you the same hope and encouragement He gave to Zerubbabel: the key to victory is not your good intentions or valiant effort, but God's own Spirit working on your behalf. And He has the power to bring you victory!

Prayer

Dear faithful Father: I am so glad Scripture isn't full of stories of people who had it all together, people who never failed or got discouraged. But I love that Scripture is full of Your assurances and promises for them and for me. You have available all I need to do Your will. You have strength and wisdom far beyond my own. Thank You for the reminder You don't expect me to do things by my might or power, but through Your own Spirit. Amen.

His Grace Really is Sufficient

"[A]ccording to the riches of his grace,
which he lavished upon us." — Ephesians 1:7b, 8a

I've had some discouraging days recently and not without reason. Scripture tells us many times not to be discouraged, but I was having a hard time climbing out of this one. But, as always, God doesn't tell us to do something without enabling us, and I found my help, once again, in His Word.

Listen to the words of 2 Corinthians 9:8: It begins with four simple words: "And God is able." Those words alone bring hope. God is able! No matter what we face, no matter how difficult the circumstances, no matter how hopeless things appear, God is able. But the verse doesn't stop there. It goes on to give us the specifics of what God is able to do. He is able to "make all grace abound" to us. All grace—not a limited supply that will run out while we still need it, but more than enough, and He'll make it abound to us. I love the word *abound*. The dictionary says it means "to be present in great quantity." God will give us great quantities of His grace.

We are also given the reason for God's outpouring of grace. This verse makes it clear it's "so that having all sufficiency in all things at all times, you may abound in every good work."

There is just nothing half-hearted about this verse. Notice the word *abound* again. He promises an abundance of grace for all we need in any and every situation.

My response to that wonderful truth was the realization I was without excuse. God wasn't just saying, "Buck up! Get over it!" He was offering me an abundant supply of His grace for my situation. These words (God's words) had just pulled the rug of discouragement right out from under my feet and placed them solidly on His promise of grace. I'll trade discouragement for abundant grace any day!

Prayer

Dear gracious God: You are so amazing and so good to us. You always have an answer for our needs, no matter what they are. And I love that You're not a stingy God. You give in abundance. Forgive me for times of discouragement and thank You for Your faithful encouragement. Amen.

God's Instructions Come with God's Enabling

"I will strengthen you, I will help you." — Isaiah 41:10c

There's an interesting account in the book of Ezekiel I find very encouraging. Ezekiel finds himself confronted with the presence of God and is overwhelmed by the glory he sees. Listen to his own words as he shares his reaction: "Such was the appearance of the likeness of the glory of the LORD. And when I saw it, I fell on my face" (Ezekiel 1:28). He fell facedown. He was overwhelmed by the glory of the One he saw and facedown was his immediate response. We find the same reaction other times in the Old Testament. Moses, Aaron, Daniel, and others all found themselves in this same facedown posture when confronted with the presence of God.

But in Ezekiel's case, he was immediately instructed to stand up on his feet. God wanted to talk to Ezekiel and wanted him upright so Ezekiel could hear what He had to say. My guess is standing wasn't an option for Ezekiel right then. He was in the presence of the Almighty and falling on his face had been an involuntary reaction. But listen to what happens next. As these instructions to stand were being given, Ezekiel tells us God's Spirit came into him and raised him to his feet (Ezekiel 2:2). God told Ezekiel to stand, and then helped him to his feet. I love that!

God may be asking you to do something way out of your comfort zone. He may even be asking you to do something you feel is impossible like standing was for Ezekiel. Let me encourage you today. God will do for you what He did for Ezekiel—offer you the help of His own Holy Spirit. God's instructions are always followed by God's enabling! It was true for Ezekiel, and it will be true for you.

Prayer

Dear God: This incident in the life of Ezekiel is so encouraging. What a wonderful picture of Your gracious help when we need it. Sometimes obedience seems beyond our ability. It's then You send Your own Spirit to enable us. You are such a good and kind God. Thank You for always helping us as we seek to be obedient to Your will. Amen.

A Clear Path

"[T]he Lord *will go before you." — Isaiah 52:12c*

In the Old Testament, the prophet Micah was assuring the Israelites of God's promise to deliver them. He offered them words of hope and the assurance God would one day restore Israel. He would gather them together and return them to their home. I'm sure those were words of great encouragement to the people of Israel. But I love the promise following that assurance.

Micah 2:13 says: "One who breaks open the way will go up before them" (NIV). God doesn't just point the way. He doesn't just lead the way. God *makes* a way. Another translation says, "The Remover of Hindrances goes before them" (Tamil). God is still The Remover of Hindrances! All those things that stand in the way of our deliverance, all those obstacles that seem like impossibilities, are cleared away by God as He leads us forward to victory.

I find such hope in these words. God goes before us. He deals with the things that make our way seem difficult or even impossible. I remember when my twin brothers were little and we were taking a walk together. They were walking ahead of me and felt it their gentlemanly duty to clear the path for me. Every twig and stone were carefully removed so their older sister didn't stumble. That's such a wonderful picture of what God is willing to do for us. One who breaks open the way, the Remover of Hindrances, will go before us. He will lead us safely home.

Micah 2:13 ends with these words: "Their king passes on before them, the LORD at their head." When you become discouraged with this journey, when you become overwhelmed by the hindrances and obstacles you face, be encouraged. The Lord is going before you, leading the way and clearing the path. He is still the Remover of Hindrances.

Prayer

Dear gracious God: I love knowing You truly are the same yesterday, today, and forever. What You did for Israel, You can do for me. No matter what the obstacle, no matter what the roadblock, You can clear the way so I can go forward on the path You have laid out for me. Thank You for going on ahead to make the way clear! Amen.

Enabler is Not a Bad Word!

"Now to him who is able…to present you blameless before the presence of his glory with great joy." — Jude 24

Enabling has earned a bad reputation in today's society. If you're called an enabler, it's definitely not a compliment. It implies you're making it easy for someone to continue in a harmful or destructive lifestyle—that you bear some of the responsibility for that person's failures. That's enabling gone bad.

But I have good news for you. *Enabler* is not a bad word! The dictionary tells us it simply means "to make (someone or something) able to do or to be something," or "to make something possible, practical, or easy." As children of God, we've been given an Enabler—One who makes it possible for us to live a lifestyle that's pleasing to God. Our Enabler, the Holy Spirit, can help us to overcome sin, to have victory over the enemy, to love people who are difficult to love. He makes it possible for us to produce fruit (or qualities) often hard for us such as love and patience, kindness and goodness, gentleness and self-control. We're often in situations when our own limited supply of these isn't enough without the enabling of God's Spirit.

But the best news of all is God also sent us His own Son as our Enabler so through His shed blood we are able to stand faultless before the throne of God. Aren't you so thankful for an Enabler who will do that?

I have a quote on my desk from the book *Beyond Humiliation* by J. Gregory Mantle that states, "My omnipotent Lord, enable me to do what, apart from Your enabling, is impossible." You see, we all need an Enabler, and God in His infinite goodness and love has sent us one.

Prayer

Dear faithful Father: You've called us to a life that is simply impossible for us apart from Your enabling. You've called us to a life that demands dependence on You and on Your help. The wonderful truth is You provide everything we need for this journey through the wonderful enabling of Your own Spirit. Thank You! Amen.

Building a Wall

"With God we shall do valiantly." — Psalm 60:12a

We've heard a lot of discussion in recent years about building a wall. Should it be built? Who will pay for it? Is it a good thing or a bad thing? The arguments and accusations have gone on for a long time and often become very heated. But controversy about building a wall is not new. In fact, there's an entire book of the Bible pretty much devoted to this very topic.

A remnant of the nation of Israel was finally able to return from exile in Babylon to their homeland. But what they found when they got there was heartbreaking. The walls of Jerusalem were broken down, and the gates had been destroyed by fire. And so, under the leadership of Nehemiah, they set about to rebuild the walls.

But not everybody was happy with what they were doing. There were those who were strongly opposed to the rebuilding of the walls and did everything they could to hinder its progress. This small group of Israelites was not only facing a daunting task but an enemy determined to defeat and discourage them.

Nehemiah's encouragement to those building the wall was this: "The God of heaven will make us prosper" (Nehemiah

2:20). Success didn't depend on them alone. He also urged his people to "remember the Lord, who is great and awesome" (Nehemiah 4:14). His advice: quit looking at the wall and quit listening to the enemy. Remember the Lord!

Are you facing a daunting task? Has God asked something of you that is difficult, that seems overwhelming? And have you heard the enemy whisper this is impossible; you can't do this or face this? Nehemiah's advice is still good. Remember the Lord. Remember the Lord who brings success. Remember the Lord who is great and awesome. And what we can't do, He can.

Prayer

Dear Almighty God: Sometimes we are so preoccupied with looking at the *wall* and forget to remember You. When we remember You—Your faithfulness, Your power, Your wisdom, Your goodness—it gives us the confidence to believe "the God of heaven will make us prosper." You did it for Nehemiah and You can do it for us. Amen.

Never Say Never

*"[H]e has granted to us his precious
and very great promises." — 2 Peter 1:4a*

There's an old adage "Never say never," and in spite of the
irony of that phrase, there is an element of truth to it. I remember saying, "I will never eat escargot!" The idea of putting
a slimy snail in my mouth and swallowing was abhorrent to
me. And I felt pretty safe in saying I would never do that. But
one day I found myself in a situation with a very gracious host
who had ordered that very thing just for me. He was anxious
for me to share the "joy" of this delicacy with him. And so,
I managed somehow to get two or three down to my horror
and the delight of my host. (I would love to say I will never eat
those again, but…"Never, say never.")

There are very few occasions when we can speak in absolutes—when we can say *never* or *always*, *all* or *nothing*. You
never know when you'll be offered escargot. But God can use
absolutes, and when He does, those words are solid and unchanging and a source of tremendous hope and comfort.

He promises *never* to leave us—not ever (Hebrews 13:5).
We will never find ourselves without His presence. He assures
us we can do *all* things through Christ—no exceptions (Phi-

lippians 4:13). He won't require something of us He can't enable us to do. And He reminds us His divine power has given us *everything* we need for life and godliness (2 Peter 1:3). We also have the assurance of His full provision. He is committed to meeting *all* our needs (Philippians 4:19). But probably the most exciting of God's absolutes is His promise that someday we will be with Him *always* and *forever* (1 Thessalonians 4:17). And that will be absolutely wonderful!

Prayer

Dear faithful God: I love the absolutes of Your Word. I love that You are able to use words like *never* and *always*, *everything* and *forever*. Those words are our hope because You are a God who is as good as His Word. We rest in that absolute truth. Amen.

Hopeful Steps

"Hope in God; for I shall again praise him,
my salvation and my God." — Psalm 42:11b

But God

*"For as the heavens are higher than the earth,
so are my ways higher than your ways and my
thoughts than your thoughts."* — Isaiah 55:9

The moment had to be overwhelming for Joseph. The men bowing before him were the same brothers who had plotted to kill him. When greed was added to their jealousy, they opted to sell him as a slave instead. And now, here they were, bowing before him asking for food. They were at his mercy.

Joseph's response was not what you might expect under the circumstances. He had found forgiveness and peace in two simple words: "But God." Joseph could look back and see God's hand in the steps of his life. He had learned the important lesson there was a "but God" even in the most awful and unfair circumstances.

As he makes himself known to his brothers, Joseph reaffirms this truth. "*But God* sent me ahead of you...So then, it was not you who sent me here, *but God*" (Genesis 45:7,8 NIV, emphasis added). And the familiar words of Genesis 50:20: "You intended to harm me, *but God* intended it for good" (NIV, emphasis added). Joseph made it clear that no matter what their intentions, this was God's plan.

You, too, may be going through a difficult time. You may feel people have mistreated you or been unfair. And while you may not be able to see it right now, there is a "but God" in your life and circumstances also.

This truth is echoed in Romans 8:28 where we are assured that for those of us who love God, He is using everything to bring about good. Even when the path is hard, when circumstances seem unfair, we can move forward in the truth there are those two simple words that make a profound difference: "but God."

Prayer

Dear all-wise God: How often we feel like our steps are at the mercy of other people or circumstances. Thank You for this reminder there is nothing in our lives that falls beyond Your reach to use and conform to Your great purpose. Thank You for the "but God" that gives us hope. Amen.

Worth the Wait

"My times are in your hand." — *Psalm 31:15a*

Have you noticed how often waiting is a part of faith? Abraham had to wait for his promised son. David was anointed as king, but spent years on the run and hiding in caves before the promise became reality. Elizabeth had to wait for a child. And the Jews waited for many long years before the Messiah came. And now we wait for the Lord's return.

Why does God keep us waiting? I don't know the answer, but what I do know is God's timing is always perfect. I love the assurance in Isaiah 60:22b: "I am the Lord; in its time I will hasten it." The NIV says, "I will do this swiftly." God is assuring us He knows what He's doing. He won't be hurried, but He won't be late.

Think of what it must have been like for the Israelites when they were slaves in Egypt. Their life was hard, but finally God sent them a deliverer and displayed His mighty power before Egypt. The Israelites were packed and ready to go, but Pharaoh refused. Over and over again they got their hopes up, and over and over again it looked like God had failed.

But God was doing something amazing. Their waiting wasn't wasted! When the time came for Israel to finally be free, the Egyptians were so anxious to get rid of them that Scripture tells us they sent them out "laden with silver and gold" (Psalm 105:37 NIV). That's silver and gold they wouldn't have had if God had answered their prayer after the first plague. God hadn't failed; He was adding on blessings while they waited.

Are you waiting for God to fulfill a promise? Are you waiting for an answer to prayer you've been bringing to God for months—maybe years? Don't give up. Don't lose hope. Your waiting won't be wasted, and God may just have some silver and gold to add to your answer.

Prayer

Dear wise God: Your ways are not our ways, and often Your timing is not our timing. But You know best. You are working while we wait and often are adding blessing that may not have come with an earlier answer. Help us to keep a quiet, trusting heart as we wait. Amen.

Now Show Me Your Glory

"We will trust in the name of the Lord our God." — Psalm 20:7b

Moses is about to embark on the monumental task of leading thousands of Israelites on the long and arduous trek to the Promised Land. It's no wonder he begs God for His presence as they travel. In fact, he as much as says, If You don't come with us, I'm not going (Exodus 33:15). And God promises He'll be with them. But then Moses proceeds to ask one more thing—something so daring, so bold we almost hold our breath waiting for God's response. Moses says, "Please show me Your glory" (Exodus 33:18).

I've always loved this account. I love the boldness of Moses, but also the graciousness of God. Most of you remember the story. Moses is covered with the hand of God and allowed to catch just a glimpse of the back of God. But Scripture tells us God promised Moses not only would His goodness pass in front of Moses, but God would also declare His name (Exodus 33:19).

Exodus 34:6 tells us as God passed in front of Moses, He proclaimed His name to be: "the Lord, the Lord, a God merciful and gracious, slow to anger, abounding in steadfast love and faithfulness!" God revealed His glory to Moses by revealing who He was—His name and His nature. And it's my guess it was those words, that declaration, that sustained Moses over and over again in the difficult years that followed. God revealed His glory to Moses to prepare and equip Him for the journey ahead.

I pray we will all be like Moses—that we will all dare to ask, "Now show me Your glory!" We need a glimpse of His glory and an understanding of His name and His nature as we go forward in our own journey.

Prayer

Dear God: You answered Moses' request by not only giving him a wonderful glimpse of Your glory, but by also revealing who You are. Moses needed to know those things about You. We need to know those things about You. They give hope and confidence to our steps. Thank You for being You. Amen.

Encouraged by Tent Pegs

"But even the hairs of your head are
all numbered." —Matthew 10:30

My husband and I are getting ready to move. Not only that, but we were just blessed with a cottage at our church camp in upstate New York. So, these days there has been much discussion (and unfortunately some sleepless nights of planning) about what goes on the truck, what gets taken to the cottage, what gets sold, and what should be given away. We have lists and lists as we work through all of this. There are still a lot of unanswered questions, but one thing we know for sure: this is God's plan for our lives.

So, what does any of this have to do with tent pegs? When God instructed Moses to build the tabernacle, He didn't just give Moses the big picture. He didn't say, "I want you to build a place where you can worship Me, so come up with some plans and get busy." He didn't even offer to just provide the architectural plans for the structure while the decorating and interior design were up to them. No, every detail was thought out by God—the color and design of the curtains, the wood used for the furnishings, what was to be covered in gold and what was to be made of bronze. The measurements and designs were all God's, right down to smallest details—even the tent pegs.

This was such a wonderful reminder to me. My husband and I are confident we're following God's plan—that the big picture has been designed by Him. But we also know we can trust this same God for all the details of that plan. When we are in His will, He will give us wisdom for even the small decisions. After all, He's a God who cares even about tent pegs.

Prayer

Dear heavenly Father: We rest in Your amazing love that knows the number of the hairs on our heads. We rest in Your amazing wisdom that knows the number of stars and even calls them each by name. Nothing is too big for You to handle, and nothing is too small for You to notice. Thank You for being a God who cares even about small details of our lives. Amen.

God Can Make a Way

"[B]ut with God all things are possible." — Matthew 19:26b

I was reading the familiar story of the suffering of the Israelites while they were slaves in Egypt when I was struck by these words, "and God commanded them [Moses and Aaron] to bring the Israelites out of Egypt." What makes those words so remarkable is Pharaoh had already made it very clear that the Israelites weren't going anywhere. In fact, if you remember, his response was to make their lives in Egypt even more miserable. At this point, the Israelites were so discouraged they didn't want to hear anything Moses or Aaron had to say to them.

Not a very promising situation, and yet, God commanded Moses and Aaron to do the impossible in spite of Pharaoh's threats. They were to lead the nation of Israel out of Egypt. Why? Because God had a plan, and God had a way, and God could do what man could not. You see, with God all things truly are possible.

Do you ever feel like God is asking you to do the impossible—to love someone who has mistreated you, to stay in a difficult situation, to break a habit that has held you in bondage for years? Be encouraged. God's commands always come with

God's enabling. He has a plan, He has a way, and He can still do the impossible.

A familiar chorus says, "God will make a way when there seems to be no way." God did it for the nation of Israel—for Moses and Aaron. He brought them out of Egypt with the entire nation of Israel. He parted the waters of the Red Sea. He fed them in the wilderness. And that same God will make a way for you too. When God asks the impossible, remember… with God all things, including your situation, are possible.

Prayer

Dear Almighty God: My situation may be different from the situation Aaron and Moses faced, but You are still the same. What You did for them, You can do for me. When things seem hopeless and a way out seems impossible, help me to trust in a God who can still make a way when there seems to be no way. Amen.

The Valley of Achor

"Those who hope in me will not be
disappointed." — Isaiah 49:23c (NIV)

Do you have a Valley of Achor? Israel did, and it was aptly named for it was a place of defeat and discouragement for them as a nation. They had just experienced a great victory as they watched the walls of Jericho fall in a dramatic display of God's power. And so, with great confidence, Israel was ready to face their next battle against the little nation of Ai. Ai was not even big enough to require all of Israel's army. They were certain of victory. But instead, Israel experienced a humiliating defeat. What had happened? Ai should have been a pushover.

What had happened was sin. Their defeat came because Achan had purposely disobeyed God, and the place where his sin was exposed and dealt with became known as the Valley of Achor—or trouble. It was a place of shame for the nation of Israel.

But it doesn't end there. In a beautiful display of God's grace, the prophet Hosea assures Israel that very place, the Valley of Achor, would one day become for them a door of hope (Hosea 2:15). I love that about God. Our places of defeat, our times of failure and discouragement are places where God offers us a door of hope—a way out to joy and victory.

Our door of hope is stated so clearly in 1 John 1:9, "If we confess our sins, he [God] is faithful and just to forgive us our sins and to cleanse us from all unrighteousness." It's a door wide open to us as God's children.

Do you have a Valley of Achor? Do you have a place where you've been defeated by sin? God doesn't intend for you to stay there, but to look up and see the door of hope He has opened wide for you—a door that leads to victory.

Prayer

Dear Father: Even in our time of failure, our Valley of Achor, we see Your grace. You offer us a door of hope with full provision for forgiveness and restoration. Help us to walk through it in full assurance of Your love. Amen.

Pondering Plunder

"[W]e are more than conquerors through him who loved us." — Romans 8:37b

Plunder is not a common part of our vocabulary—or our experience. We simply don't do a lot of plundering in this day and age. However, that wasn't the case in Bible times. The PS to every battle won was the plunder—cows, sheep, gold, silver, even people who were all considered the rightful gain of the victor.

This morning I was reading one of Judah's battles in the Old Testament. They were a small nation, and Scripture tells us they were facing a vast army and three hundred chariots (2 Chronicles 14:9), which gave the enemy a decided advantage over Judah. But Judah cried out to God, and He gave them a great and glorious victory...and lots of plunder. They went home victorious and wealthy.

I remember talking to a woman at church recently who was facing overwhelming circumstances. Much like Judah, she was facing forces that far outnumbered her. We were encouraged as we read Scripture after Scripture encouraging us to believe God still promises great and glorious victories against the enemy. But as I continued to read, I realized a wonderful truth.

God also wants us to come away with plunder. He wants us to gain things of great value from our battles—not sheep or cattle, but things of eternal worth. He adds riches to our lives when we experience His victory—an increase in faith, a closer relationship with Him, a glimpse of His mighty power, a renewed sense of His love and care, and much more.

I'm so glad the days of plundering aren't over. The enemy is real, the battle often difficult, but God still gives victory. We may come home battle-worn and weary, but we can also come home with great wealth, the spiritual plunder that rightfully belongs to the victors.

Prayer

Dear victorious Lord: We also face battles. And like the kings in Bible days, we look to You for our victory. But I love this reminder there is more than just victory for us: there is plunder. There is wealth that comes from victory. Thank You! Amen.

A Faithful Walking Companion

"[H]is mercies never come to an end; they are new every morning; great is your faithfulness." — Lamentations 3:22b–23

As Pure Gold

"I will never leave you nor forsake you." — Hebrews 13:5b

Amy Carmichael shares a wonderful story of taking some children to visit a goldsmith. As Amy relates the process of refining the gold, we see a clear picture of God's work of refining in our own lives.

As often as I've shared this story, I found a wonderful new truth recently. It was a side comment in parentheses, but still an important reminder. Amy Carmichael shared that the goldsmith never leaves the crucible once it's in the fire. When he begins the refining process, the gold is never left unattended. He watches over every step of the process.

This is also true for us. When we are "in the fire" of suffering, our Refiner will never leave us. He has a purpose for the flames and will stay right there to see they work for our good. What was literally true for Shadrach, Meshach, and Abednego is also true for us. God will be with us through the fiery trials.

This is more than just a nice thought from Amy Carmichael's story. This truth is solidly backed by Scripture. Psalm 46:1 assures us "God is…a very present help in trouble." He never leaves the gold once it's in the fire. Both the flames and the gold are under His loving and watchful eye.

I find such encouragement in these words. We will never be left unattended in the flames as God lovingly accomplishes His purpose. As Job declared, "when he has tried me, I shall come out as gold" (Job 23:10b).

I especially love the end of Amy's story when she asked the goldsmith how he can tell when the gold is pure. His answer is such a powerful reminder of God's goal for us. "When I can see my face in it, then it is pure." And God will stay right with us until then.

Prayer

Dear loving Father: What a comfort to be assured of Your presence—especially during the difficult days when we are being tested and refined. I love that You never walk away and come back when we're done but stay with us every minute. Thank You for the promise of Your very present help. Amen.

A Coat with a Belt

"You have led in your steadfast love the people
whom you have redeemed." — Exodus 15:13a

Did you know a coat with a belt can be an important part of a mother's wardrobe? It certainly was for me. It was my solution for safely maneuvering across streets and busy parking lots with a baby and two very small children. I only had two hands to care for three of them. My solution was to carry the youngest while the other two had strict instructions to each hang on to an end of the belt on my coat. I was committed to their safety and their care, so we didn't move until their pudgy little hands were firmly attached to my belt with a stern warning not to let go. I knew as long as they held on, they would be right by my side, only go where I led them, and be safe.

Actually, God had that idea long before I did. When I was maneuvering through a very scary time of life, I found these reassuring words in Scripture. "Righteousness will be his belt and faithfulness the sash around his waist" (Isaiah 11:5 NIV). All of a sudden, I was the child and my heavenly Father was offering me His belt and saying, "hold on!" I knew as long as I did, I would be by His side, and He would guide my steps even through uncertain times. His righteousness and faithfulness would keep me safe. He loved me and was committed to my care and safety.

What are you facing today? Are you unsure of your next step? Are you in the middle of circumstances that are frightening? Look up...you'll see the end of a belt and hear a loving Father say, "Hang on, you'll be okay."

Prayer

Dear loving Father: My coat with a belt was motivated by love and concern for my precious children. Your belt and sash are because of that same love and concern for us. Thank You for the safety we find in hanging on to Your belt of righteousness and sash of faithfulness. You are a good God. Amen.

When You Can't Find God

"For the eyes of the Lord are on the righteous." — 1 Peter 3:12a

Have you ever felt like you just can't find God? You're not alone. Job had the same struggle. Job had experienced unbelievable suffering. He lost his possessions and wealth; he lost his own children; and he was afflicted with agonizing boils from head to foot. He had experienced deep suffering and heartache. However, in Job 23:3 we hear the real anguish of his heart as he cries out, "Oh, that I knew where I might find him." In the midst of Job's suffering, he yearns to talk to God, to share his heart, to find God's answers, but he can't find Him.

It's not because Job hasn't searched. He tells us he's gone to the east and God isn't there. He can't find Him in the west. And he can't see Him in the north or catch a glimpse of Him in the south. He has looked everywhere!

While our suffering may never compare to Job's, many of us can identify with the sense that in the midst of our worst times, we can't seem to find God no matter where we look.

Job himself offers us this hope: He says in essence: "I may not be able to find God, but He knows where I am. I can't see Him, but He still sees me" (Job 23:10 paraphrase). And Job found tremendous comfort in that truth.

Most of us know how the story ends. God greatly blessed the later years of Job's life with wealth and cattle and family. But I think the real blessing is found in Job 42:5 when Job says, "but now my eye sees you." Job finally found God.

Prayer

Dear faithful Father: What a comfort to remember during those times when it seems You're nowhere to be found, You still see us. You know exactly where we are and have Your loving eyes fixed on us. And thank You for the assurance these times don't last forever. Like Job, the day will come when we have the joy of sensing Your presence again and the glorious hope of someday seeing You face-to-face where we will never lose sight of You again. Amen.

A God Who Listens

"[F]rom the first day that you set your heart to understand and humbled yourself before your God, your words have been heard." — Daniel 10:12

One of the very first things we learn about God is that He speaks. In creation, He spoke things into existence. It's apparent He had conversations with Adam and Eve. He spoke to Israel through the prophets, and He speaks today through His Word and His Spirit. What a wonderful thing to have a God who speaks—who communicates with us.

But that's only part of it. We also have a God who listens. In fact, He's a very good listener. The psalmist declares in Psalm 116 that one of the reasons he loves the Lord is because God listens to him. He says God "inclines" or turns His ear toward him. I love that imagery. Can't you just picture God leaning over, intent on hearing every word on the psalmist's heart. One of the blessings God promised to Israel was that while they were still speaking, He would hear. No need to repeat; no need to get His attention. He was listening…and He still is!

One of the most common complaints I hear when counseling women is their husband doesn't listen to them, or their teenagers no longer pay any attention to what they're saying.

Listening is important in any relationship, and we have a God who listens! We have a God who is willing to incline His ear to us—to give us His full attention as we share our hearts and needs with Him.

I hope you agree with the psalmist. I hope you also have the absolute assurance that when you speak to God, He listens and listens carefully. What a truly wonderful reason to love Him!

Prayer

Dear Father: This is a wonderful and reassuring truth. We've all been with people who don't give us their full attention when we talk to them. But You incline Your ear to us. You give us Your full attention because You love us and love to hear what's on our hearts. Thank You for the assurance that gives. When we pray, You listen. Amen.

A Good God

"Oh, taste and see that the Lord is good!" — *Psalm 34:8*

I've been thinking a lot lately about the goodness of God. Scripture makes it clear that among all His other qualities—His omnipotence, His unfailing love, His wisdom, grace, and mercy—is this wonderful quality of His goodness. We don't hear that quality mentioned as often. It's seldom the topic of a sermon or devotional, but it's an important part of God's character and has great impact on our lives. He is good. He is good in His nature, and He is good at what He does.

The first response we ever see from God in Scripture is an acknowledgment that what He had done was good (Genesis 1:10). He looked at what He had made and was pleased. He declared it to be good. And what He does is still good. Romans 12:2 describes God's will—God's purpose and plan for us—as good and acceptable and perfect.

God is not only good in what He does, His own nature is one of goodness. He is a good God and that matters greatly to us. If He were all-powerful, but not good, we would live in fear. If He were unchanging and eternal, but not good, we would be without hope. If He were all-seeing and all-knowing, but not good, we would have no peace or joy.

His goodness gives us confidence in all His other wonderful qualities. It puts our hearts at rest and our minds at ease. We are under the care of a good God.

God's goodness may not be sung about or preached about as much as some of His other qualities, but I, for one, am so thankful we have a good God. I rest in the fact that what He does is good, and I rejoice in the truth that He is, by nature, a good God.

Prayer

Dear good God: We often take Your goodness for granted, but we are surrounded by evidence You are a good, good God. There's a certain irony in the fact that the greatest display of Your goodness is when You were covered in my sins. Forgive us for sometimes taking Your goodness for granted. We love that You're a good God. Amen.

An Empty Folder

*"If we confess our sins, he is faithful and just
to forgive us our sins." — 1 John 1:9*

I am in no way a computer expert. And I'm so thankful you don't have to understand computers to use them. However, I, like so many others, find them becoming more and more an integral part of my life.

A recent experience with my computer served as a wonderful reminder of a spiritual truth. In cleaning out some old documents, I came across a folder I thought was long gone. It was one I didn't need any more and was surprised to find that apparently it had been hidden away somewhere in the mysterious depths of my hard drive. I decided to open it to look again at the contents, only to discover that it was empty. The folder was there, the name was the same, but everything in it was gone.

So it is with us. The folder in our life marked *sin* is empty—it's been wiped clean. However, we have a very sneaky enemy who will occasionally bring up the folder and show it to us to remind us of our past, of our failures and sinful acts. We see the folder cover and it looks convincing. We once again feel the shame and remorse of past failures. But what the enemy doesn't want us to do is to boldly open it to reveal it's empty.

There's nothing there for him to use to condemn us. It's been gloriously and completely wiped clean with the blood of Jesus Christ! It doesn't matter if the folder's still hidden away somewhere in our hearts—the contents are gone!

There was a chorus we used to sing in Sunday School, "Gone, gone, gone, gone; Yes, my sins are gone." It was a simple chorus, but a profound truth. Next time the enemy shows you a folder marked *sin*—no matter what the sin—boldly open it and remind him that everything in it is "G-O-N-E — gone!"

Prayer

Dear gracious God: The psalmist said if You kept a record of our sins none of us could stand.* With forgiveness comes an empty folder. It doesn't matter what was in there; it's empty and clean. Thank You. You truly are faithful and just and will forgive our sins. Amen.

*Psalm 130:3

Making Assumptions

"Let us hold fast the confession of our hope without wavering, for he who promised is faithful." — Hebrews 10:23

Have you ever assumed someone would do something they promised, only to be disappointed? Or had a friendship that has failed to be what you had hoped and believed it would be? What about the assumption a product would be just as it was advertised only to discover it was far less than what was promised? I think most of us can answer yes to these questions. We've all had experience with failed assumptions.

I remember when, as a very little girl, a woman in our church promised to get me some little toy. Week after week I waited, but it never came. I'm sure she simply forgot, but I didn't and was very disappointed. I think this is still such a clear memory because it was probably the first time I experienced that let down—the disappointment that comes with a misplaced assumption.

But I have good news today. We can assume on God. We can be sure He keeps His word. We can be certain His promises won't fail, and His grace and mercy will never diminish. We can assume all God says He is and all He promises He'll do. God keeps His word and will not fail!

We can assume when God says He'll never leave us, He really won't. When He promises to supply all our needs according to His riches in glory, He will. And when He assures us our present suffering is temporary and will someday be replaced with a glory beyond compare, we can assume that's exactly what will happen. We can assume on God.

People fail, products aren't all they're promised to be, but God never, never fails! He will always keep His word…and we can assume on that!

Prayer

Dear faithful Father: People fail and sometimes that's disappointing or painful. What a comfort to know we have a God who will never fail, never go back on a promise, and will always keep His word. We can assume You are who You say You are and will do what You say You will do. What a wonderful assumption! Amen.

Steps of Worship

"*Oh come, let us worship and bow down; let us kneel before the Lord, our Maker!*" — *Psalm 95:6*

A Gift of Dandelions

"[M]an looks on the outward appearance, but the
Lord looks on the heart." — 1 Samuel 16:7c

When my son was little, I overheard him tell someone his mommy's favorite flower was the dandelion. I guess my genuine reaction of delight when given a hand-picked bouquet of those weeds, usually clasped in a grubby little fist, led him to believe they surely must be my favorite.

However, what I did love were yellow roses—pale yellow roses. But my children weren't capable of getting me roses. They didn't have the means or the ability. Dandelions were free and, unfortunately, were available in abundance in our backyard.

When my children brought me dandelions, I didn't really look at the flowers, I looked at the child. What I saw was the love that prompted the gift and the genuine desire to please. It was the heart of the giver that made that handful of flowers so precious. I loved those little bouquets because they were an honest expression of my children's love to the best of their limited resources and ability.

I often think of that during times of worship. I do love the Lord, deeply love the Lord, but so often I feel like my attempts to convey my love in genuine worship fall so far short of what

He deserves. And then I remember grubby little fists full of dandelions. The Lord doesn't insist on yellow roses if dandelions are the very best I can offer.

I'm so thankful when I offer God my worship, He sees the heart behind the gift and accepts the faltering, inadequate words with joy and love. He deserves so much more, but who knows…maybe dandelions are His favorite flower.

Prayer

Dear Father: My outward expressions of worship are often not an accurate reflection of my heart. I love You and know You deserve flawless and endless worship. I can offer You neither of those, but may I never bring You less than my best, even if my best is a fistful of dandelions. Amen.

Four Simple Words

*"Worship the LORD in the splendor
of holiness." — 1 Chronicles 16:29c*

Do you ever struggle with prayer? Do you sometimes have trouble staying focused? Or do you ever wonder how to pray—or what to pray? Are there times when you don't sense God's presence or your faith is so small? I think all of us have struggled with these things from time to time. We know we should pray. We honestly want to pray. But sometimes we find prayer so hard.

Years ago, I was given some advice about prayer that has been such a help and encouragement. It's just four simple words, but words that have helped me probably more than any book I've ever read on prayer. They are simply: "Always begin with worship."

Christ demonstrated this principle in the Lord's Prayer. He began His prayer with these words: "Our Father in heaven, hallowed be your name" (Matthew 6:9). Jesus began with worship. He began by acknowledging God's name was hallowed—holy, sacred, revered. Before He asked, He worshipped.

When we begin with worship, we take the attention off our needs and ourselves and focus on God. As we express worship to God, our hearts are reminded of who He is, of all He's promised; we remember His great love; we think of His power and His faithfulness. There is nothing like a glimpse of the Almighty to increase our faith.

But something else happens when we begin with worship. As we're in God's presence, His Spirit begins to direct our prayers, and we find ourselves praying according to His will and purposes. The Spirit helps us because "we do not know what to pray for as we ought" (Romans 8:26).

Four simple words with profound impact. When you don't know how to pray or what to ask when God seems distant—always begin with worship and let Him lead from there!

Prayer

Dear Holy God: To begin our prayers with worship is not a magic formula. We begin with worship simply because You are worthy of our worship. Sometimes we are so focused on our needs we forget the importance of focusing first on You. Thank You for these four simple words that bring focus to our time in Your presence. Amen.

A Gift in Return

*"If you then…know how to give good gifts to your children,
how much more will your Father who is in heaven give
good things to those who ask him!" — Matthew 7:11*

This incident took place at Christmas time, but it's much more a story of God's response to our worship than it is about Christmas.

Sam was asked to play the Christ child in the Christmas program years ago. Most scholars believe the wise men came later when Mary and Joseph were in a home and Jesus was a toddler, so our church decided to depict it that way. The scene was simple—rough wood walls, a simple table with a bowl of fruit on it, and Mary and Joseph sitting quietly with real life toddler Sam as Jesus nearby.

Sam looked up wide-eyed as the wise men arrived, then grinned when he recognized one of them as his older brother. The first of the magi knelt in worship and presented Sam (the Christ child) with a gift. Sam took it, and then immediately reached up on the table and offered his guest a piece of fruit. This unrehearsed response on Sam's part was repeated for each of the wise men. They came bearing gifts but left with a gift given in return.

What a picture of worship. We come to worship. Sometimes it's a difficult and long journey from our own heartaches or problems, from difficult circumstances, and disappointments, but we choose to come—to make the journey, to bow before our Savior, and to offer him the gift of our worship. But always, when genuine worship takes place, we come away with a gift given by Christ in return. It may be peace needed for a hardship, joy lacking because of stress and busyness, but whatever the gift, it has been chosen by Christ specifically for you.

Worship is not only for Christmas. I trust you'll make time all year to "come and worship." The journey is always worth it. And as you offer the gift of worship to the One who alone is worthy, He will bless you with a gift in return!

Prayer

Dear Holy God: This is so much more than a sweet story. There's a truth demonstrated here for all Your children. You are a generous and loving God, and when we come to You with the gift of our worship, You reach out and give us exactly what we need in return. Thank You for using a little boy to remind us of this truth. Amen.

A Little Trembling is
a Good Thing

*"To whom will you compare me? Or who is
my equal?" — Isaiah 40:25 (NIV)*

God's people had backslidden. All over Israel and Judah were places of worship and altars to the gods of other nations while the living God of Israel was forgotten. What had happened? How could this take place among God's own people?

I think we find the answer in questions God asks through the prophet Jeremiah. "Do you not fear me?...Do you not tremble before me?" (Jeremiah 5:22). In other words, Israel had lost their sense of reverence and awe in the presence of God (Jeremiah 2:19).

So many things in our relationship with God fall into their rightful place when we remember to be in awe of Him—when we remember His overwhelming greatness, His utterly pure holiness, His unequaled power and might.

A lot has changed since Jeremiah's day. Our approach to God has changed because of the cross, but God hasn't changed. We may come into His presence "with confidence" (Hebrews

10:19), but it's still appropriate to do a little trembling. It's our awe of God that leads us to genuine worship. It's a sense of trembling in His presence that motivates us to obedience. It's standing in the presence of His overwhelming greatness that increases our faith, and it's a glimpse of His heart that deepens our love.

Israel had not forgotten to worship. They had places of worship all over the land. But they had forgotten the utter greatness of their God. They had forgotten He alone was God, the true God, their God—majestic and holy, glorious and mighty. God got right to the heart of Israel's problem. They had forgotten to fear God and tremble in His presence.

Let's not be like the Israelites. When we come into God's presence in worship, let's remember we are in the presence of indescribable greatness and holiness. When we approach God in worship, a little trembling is always appropriate.

Prayer

Dear great and awesome God: There is such a dichotomy in coming into Your presence. We are lovingly welcomed as Your child, but we need to remember who our Father is and never lose our rightful sense of awe and wonder in Your presence. The more we know You, the more we understand trembling is appropriate as we bow ourselves in humble worship. You alone are worthy! Amen.

Mouth-Heart Coordination

"Let the words of my mouth and the meditation of my heart be acceptable in your sight." — Psalm 19:14a

We often hear people referring to the importance of hand-eye coordination. That simply means our hands respond consistently and appropriately with what our eyes see. My grandson has recently learned to juggle—an impressive display of hand-eye coordination, and one he loves to demonstrate.

Scripture doesn't mention hand-eye coordination, but it does have a lot to say about mouth-heart coordination. God cares very much that what comes out of our mouths is consistent with what is in our hearts. Jeremiah complained to God about Israel's problem with this very thing. He says, "You are always on their lips but far from their hearts" (Jeremiah 12:2b NIV).

In another Scripture, Jeremiah expresses that same truth again. "You are near in their mouth and far from their heart." Israel was lacking in mouth-heart coordination. Their mouths were saying all the right things, but it was not consistent with what God knew was in their hearts.

This obviously wasn't just an Old Testament condition. In speaking of the Pharisees, Jesus said, "This people honors me with their lips, but their heart is far from me" (Matthew

15:8). Jesus wasn't impressed with their words because He knew their hearts.

How is your mouth-heart coordination? Do you go to church or Bible study and say all the right words, quote the right Scripture, sing words of praise and worship, but all from a heart that is cold or indifferent to the things of God? God makes it very clear it's the heart that matters to Him. He wants our words of worship and praise to come from the overflow of a heart that loves Him and obeys Him. You may never have the hand-eye coordination necessary to juggle, but you can examine your heart so your mouth-heart coordination brings joy to your heavenly Father.

Prayer

Dear heavenly Father: We know man looks on the outward appearance, and so often we do things for the benefit of the people watching. But it doesn't matter how high our hands are raised in worship if they aren't a reflection of genuine worship taking place in our heart. Give us perfect mouth-heart coordination for Your glory, I pray. Amen.

Come and Worship

"Oh come, let us worship and bow down." — Psalm 95:6a

When we hear the phrase "come and worship," our minds immediately go to Christmas. But I've been thinking a lot about the *coming* part of worship recently. The shepherds came to Bethlehem to see the Christ child and fell down and worshipped. The wise men traveled many miles and many days to find the new King and bowed before Him in worship. What the Lord has been teaching me is true worship always takes place when we take the time to come into His presence.

Imagine if the shepherds had just stayed in their fields and discussed all they had seen and heard from the angels. They probably would have had some very sincere and meaningful conversations, but they wouldn't have had worship.

Imagine if the wise men had stayed in their own countries and written scholarly reports on the star and its significance. They may have written some important documents, but they wouldn't have worshipped.

I wonder how often we try to worship without taking the time to first make the journey into His presence. For the shepherds and the wise men, it was a physical journey; for us it's a journey of the heart. For the shepherds and wise men, it led to a baby; for us it leads to a victorious and risen Savior.

The shepherd's response to the angel's message wasn't, "Let's go and worship." Their response was, "Let's go and see." And when they arrived, what they saw brought them to their knees in worship. They worshipped because they were in the presence of God, even if God was wrapped in swaddling clothes.

Come and worship is a year-round invitation. We often miss the best worship by not first taking the journey from our everyday circumstances, from the things that distract us, to come into the presence of our amazing and wonderful God. For He is worthy of our worship and definitely worth the trip.

Prayer

Dear Holy God: You are the reason for our worship. Worship is not merely singing a song or praying. It's entering into Your presence to express our love and adoration to You in person. You are worthy of our worship, and You are worth the journey. Amen.

Worship is More Than Music

"[T]hat God may be all in all." — 1 Corinthians 15:28b

Sometimes it's not a deep theological argument or doctrinal debate that has the greatest impact, but a few simple words. That was my experience as I read, "that in everything he might be preeminent" (Col. 1:18c). Simple words, but profound truth I knew needed to be the reality of every aspect of my life. The Amplified Bible, Classic Edition puts it like this: "that He alone in everything *and* in every respect might occupy the chief place [stand first and be preeminent]." Or as the NASB expresses it: "that He Himself will come to have first place in everything."

For me this was a selah moment, one where I needed to sit and think about the implication of these words. In a generic sense, I would say immediately Christ was first (preeminent) in my life, which is certainly my desire and prayer. But the challenge of these words is that He is to be preeminent in "all things" with no exceptions. I began to think about specific areas of my life and ask, "Does He truly have first place in this area, in this situation, in these circumstances?" And soon the question became a prayer: "Lord, please, in this area of need have supremacy, in these circumstances come first." You see,

I have a long history of struggling with self, with liking to be first myself, so this was a necessary and important time of allowing the Spirit to search my heart.

Before you wonder what this has to do with worship, let me explain. According to Paul, this actually has everything to do with worship. In Romans 12:1, Paul reminds us that giving ourselves completely to God as a living sacrifice is an act of "spiritual worship," one that is "holy and acceptable to God."

Just a few simple words, but our response to those words can become our greatest act of worship.

Prayer

Dear Holy God: We often narrow the concept of worship down to songs and prayers. You've made it clear that absolute surrender of ourselves to You is also an act of worship—one that adds significance to our other acts of worship. May we add our lives to our voices in an act of love and worship to the One who is worthy. Amen.

Stepping Toward the Goal

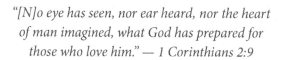

"[N]o eye has seen, nor ear heard, nor the heart of man imagined, what God has prepared for those who love him." — 1 Corinthians 2:9

Run Your Race

"I have finished the race, I have kept the faith.
Henceforth there is laid up for me the crown
of righteousness." — 2 Timothy 4:7b–8a

My niece accomplished a remarkable feat a few years ago. She ran a fifty-mile marathon. Yes, a fifty-mile marathon! There was one point in the last few miles of the race when the path led up a steep incline on a mountain road. Cherie clearly remembers crying out in exhaustion and frustration: "Who would do this? Who would plan an uphill course at the end of a grueling fifty-mile race?" And yet she pushed on.

Why? Why didn't she just pick an easier path—a level stretch of road or a shaded more comfortable route? The answer was simple: this was the race laid out for her. Cherie didn't get to pick the route; her job was to persevere along the path chosen for her to run.

Hebrews 12:1 mentions this very same thing. The writer encourages and challenges believers to "run with endurance the race that is set before us." We don't get to choose only the easy or comfortable paths. Sometimes, like Cherie, we find ourselves crying out, "Who would do this? Who would include this hard part in the race I'm running?"

But Cherie kept going, even over the hard parts, because her goal was to finish the race laid out for her. She knew at the finish line were family members waiting for her, to welcome her and express their love and pride in her accomplishment.

We also have a finish line ahead in the race that's marked out for us. Waiting for us are friends and family, but even more, there's a Savior who will be there to welcome us. And to hear Him say, "Well done!" will make every step worth it.

Prayer

Dear Father: Sometimes we get tired of running. Sometimes we don't like the path that's been laid out for us. But there's a time when all of this will be so worth it—a time when we cross the finish line and fall into Your arms. Until then, may we "run with endurance" the race laid out for us. Amen.

A Marvelous Reaction

*"Behold, he is coming with the clouds, and
every eye will see him." — Revelation 1:7*

Did you know the Bible tells us exactly how we will respond when the Lord returns? Second Thessalonians 1:10 gives us a clear picture of what our reaction will be when we catch a glimpse of the Lord for the first time. It says He will be "marveled at among all who have believed."

Marvel is defined as something that causes wonder—the quality of exciting, amazed admiration or rapt attention or astonishment at something awesomely mysterious. What a perfect description of our response to the Lord's return.

Some of our family recently went to Niagara Falls for the first time. They had all seen pictures of the Falls; they had even seen it on television so they knew something of its power and splendor, but nothing totally prepared them for their first glimpse of it in person. What was their response? They stood and marveled!

That's how it will be for us. We understand Christ will come in a display of splendor and power like nothing ever seen before. We know He's majestic and glorious and holy. We've seen Him revealed in Scripture, we've experienced moments of His presence, but my guess is nothing can ever totally prepare us for our first glimpse of Him in person. We will be among those who stand and marvel—not because Scripture tells us too, not because that's how we think we should respond, but because that will be our involuntary reaction to the awesome reality of His presence. The very sight of Him will evoke a sense of marvel we have never felt before, and we will gaze at our returning King with amazed admiration, with rapt attention and astonishment at One who is awesomely mysterious and yet wonderfully familiar.

I'm looking forward to being there with you that day, but don't expect me to notice you. I'll be too busy gazing with marvel at our wonderful returning Lord!

Prayer

Dear glorious King: I find it hard to fully express my anticipation for the moment when we finally see You face-to-face. You truly will be a sight to behold as we all stand in awe and wonder, marveling at the very sight of You. "What a day, glorious day, that will be!" Amen.

Even to the End

"I will not leave you or forsake you." — Joshua 1:5c

Do the headlines ever scare you? Do you ever get discouraged watching the evening news? It can be very unsettling, even frightening, to listen to what is going on in the world—even what is going on in our own country. More and more of our world is in turmoil. These are definitely days of wars and rumors of wars.

But there's a difference when you hear Christians discussing world events, especially the volatile situation in the Middle East. Someone almost always mentions that it certainly seems like these must be the last days. And there are understandable reasons for that response. There truly are many things that have happened in recent years in fulfillment of prophecy.

The hope of Christ's soon return truly is encouraging and offers great hope, but what about in the meantime? What about these days we're facing as things worsen daily in so many areas of the world? What happens while we wait?

I found some wonderful words of encouragement in Scripture recently. I was raised in a denomination with a strong emphasis on missions, and so the words of Matthew 28:19 and 20 are very familiar. Often referred to as the Great Commission,

197

these were some of Christ's last words to His disciples, and they give us clear instructions as to what we're to be doing as we wait for the Lord's return. But the words that follow are what stood out for me. Jesus goes on to say, "And behold, I am with you always, to the end of the age." God promises us His presence right to the very last minute we're here on this earth. I find great comfort in that.

What a wonderful reminder! God Himself not only assures us of His return (and maybe soon), but He also assures us there's one thing certain in these uncertain days. He will be with us! And that's great news.

Prayer

Dear Father: It is always comforting for a child to have their parent with them during a frightening time, and You have promised us that same comfort. The hope of Your return is wonderful, but the promise of Your presence until that day offers us great assurance. We don't know what the days ahead hold, but we know we won't face them alone. You are a wonderful Father! Amen.

Just a Hint

*"[N]o eye has seen, nor ear heard, nor the heart
of man imagined, what God has prepared for
those who love him." — 1 Corinthians 2:9*

Have you ever had someone give you a hint about something, maybe a gift or a surprise? They don't tell you everything, just a little piece of information to keep you interested. The dictionary defines *hint* as "a very small amount of something."

In chapter 26 of Job we have an amazing description of the might and power of God. It's beyond the scope of our imaginations to grasp a mind great enough to plan our universe and the immense power to bring it into being. Then Job reminds us, "these are but the outer fringe of his works; how faint the whisper we hear of him!" (Job 26:14 NIV). Job is reminding us that what we know of God's greatness is just a hint, a very small picture of who God really is.

We find another hint of God's utter greatness in 2 Thessalonians 2:8. Referring to the end times it says, "And then the lawless one will be revealed, whom the Lord Jesus will kill with the breath of His mouth and bring to nothing by the appearance of his coming." Imagine that! God's power is so great that with just a breath He is able to defeat the enemy, and the very splendor of His presence will utterly destroy him.

I love the worship chorus reminding us we stand in awe of God because He's simply too marvelous for words. Right now, our limited minds and hearts can only handle a hint of how truly marvelous God is.

Remember the definition of hint: "a very small amount of something." Or as Job said, "Just a whisper." Someday we won't need any more hints, and what cannot be conveyed in words will be seen and known in reality. And in that moment, as we see the One who truly is too marvelous for words, we will stand in utter awe.

Prayer

Dear awesome God: Even the hints we get about You are enough for us to stand in awe of You. But someday, there will be no more hints, just the reality of Your holy and glorious presence. I'm sure in that moment, words will be totally inadequate, and we will find ourselves flat on our faces in worship. Until that day, thank You for the hints. Amen.

No Regrets

"For you have need of endurance, so that when you have done the will of God you may receive what is promised." — Hebrews 10:36

My husband and I enjoy following college basketball. Our two favorite teams are Duke and Syracuse, and we're united in cheering for them—unless they're playing each other. At that point my loyalty lies completely with the Syracuse Orange, and he…well, he's for those other guys. We definitely sit on opposite ends of the couch during that game.

A few years ago, Mason Plumlee was the center for Duke and was an impressive player. But he was also an impressive young man. (And this compliment comes from a Syracuse fan.) His senior year he declared he wanted to end the year with no regrets. In other words, he wanted to end his college basketball career knowing he had played his best and given it his all. It didn't mean he would make every shot and defend every play, but it did mean he would follow the game plan of his coach and remain faithful to his commitment as a Duke basketball player.

No regrets! I was very struck by those words—especially in light of the Lord's return. It seems as though each day brings us more evidence His return could be very soon, and I want to be like Mason Plumlee. I want to end my time here on Earth with no regrets. I want to know I've persevered and been faithful to the call of God on my life. I want to know I've been obedient to His will and His plans. I want to know I've remained faithful to my commitment to the kingdom of God.

So, thank you, Mason. Thank you for the challenge of your words. I hope as you look back on your years as a Duke basketball player, you have no regrets. But even more, I pray that as children of God we live in such a way we can end our journey here with no regrets. I pray we will have persevered and kept our eyes on the goal so we can hear, "Well done!"

Prayer

Dear heavenly Father: Scripture has so clearly laid out the game plan for us. We are given clear guidance as to our place in Your kingdom. This is so much more serious than a basketball game. This is our one shot at life on Earth. Help us to live in a way that honors You so we can end our days here with no regrets for Your glory. Amen.

Does God Smile?

"Splendor and majesty are before him; strength and joy are in his place." — 1 Chronicles 16:27

Does God smile? That's a question I was asked recently. I'm sure Jesus smiled while He was here on Earth. I can't imagine children being drawn to Him if He continually had a stern, unsmiling expression. And don't you think He smiled when Peter jumped out of the boat to walk toward Him? What about when Lazarus came out of the tomb? My guess is, as Lazarus' body was unwrapped, one of the first things he saw was the smiling face of the One who loved him—Jesus. And I wonder if His smile encouraged Mary as she lovingly poured out the contents of her alabaster box to anoint Him.

But what about God? Does He smile? He is so often represented as a stern being, but we are created in His image, and He created us with the ability to smile—to experience joy and happiness. Listen to these words in Zephaniah 3:16–17. "Fear not, O Zion; let not your hands grow weak. The LORD Your God is in your midst, a mighty one who will save; he will rejoice over you with gladness; he will quiet you by his love; he will exult over you with loud singing." I find it hard to imagine a God who takes great delight in us and rejoices over us with singing, wouldn't be smiling.

We also know there is rejoicing in heaven when someone becomes a child of God (Luke 15:7). It seems to me there must be a lot of smiling going on then. The Bible is full of verses that talk about joy and rejoicing. It's hard to imagine those would come from an unsmiling God.

Some wonderful day, we will see God face-to-face, and if we've been faithful to Him on this journey, we may hear Him say, "Well done, good and faithful servant" (Matt. 25:21). I strongly suspect when we look up as He speaks those words, we'll see a God with a big smile on His face.

Prayer

Dear loving Father: I want to give You many, many reasons to smile. I want to bring You joy. I want to delight Your heart. And someday, I want to see Your smiling face as You welcome me home. Amen.

And God Said

"[T]he sheep follow him, for they know his voice." — John 10:4b

Our first glimpse of God in Scripture is a glorious display of the power of words. We are introduced to a Creator God who simply spoke things into being. "And God said…" and it was. Wouldn't you love to have been there? Wouldn't you love to have heard God's words and watched in wonder as those words brought sun and stars, grass and trees, fish and birds into existence? Imagine being there to hear Him speak again as He looked at the results of His words and said, "This is good!"

What an amazing display of the power of God's voice, but His voice did not remain silent. God's voice was heard even more clearly through His own Son. John declares "the Word became flesh and dwelt among us" (John 1:14). God's voice came to Earth—first in the cry of a newborn baby, and later His voice spoke healing and forgiveness to those in need. That same voice invited children to come to Him and called for Lazarus to come out of the tomb. And His voice spoke words that changed all of history as He cried out, "It is finished" (John 19:30). In that moment of anguish, God's Son, the Word, declared the purpose for God's voice to be heard on Earth had been accomplished.

God continues to speak through His Spirit and through Scripture. What an amazing privilege and help to have His voice so readily available to us. But there will come a day for each of us when God's voice will lovingly tell us we have taken our last step in the journey of life. That day is the culmination of our journey made up of all our big steps and little steps. But the final step we take will lead straight into His arms as we hear Him say, "Welcome home!"

Prayer

Dear Father: This journey of life we're on has a goal. And that goal is to be forever with You. Whether we hear the trumpet announce Your arrival, or You gently call us to Yourself, our journey will be complete, and the end of our steps will be glorious! Amen.

Endnotes

1. James Herriot, *All Things Bright and Beautiful* (New York: St. Martin's Press, 1973), 376.

2. A. W. Tozer, *The Pursuit of God* (Camp Hill, PA: Christian Publications, 1982), 15.

3. Ibid. 40.

4. Gladys Taber, *Harvest of Yesterdays* (New York: J. P. Lippincott Co., 1976) .

5. Oswald Chambers, *My Utmost for His Highest.*

About the Author

Esther Lovejoy is a frequent retreat and conference speaker with over thirty years of ministry experience. Her passion is to encourage women in their personal journey with God through her speaking and writing.

Esther is a contributing author to *Inspired by Tozer*, published by Regal in 2011, and the author of *The Sweet Side of Suffering: Recognizing God's Best When Facing Life's Worst and An Unnatural Beauty: Rediscovering the Beauty of Holiness.* She enjoys sharing her own journey with God on her blog, ViewFromTheSparrowsNest.com.

Answers, gifts...
love and promises...

Abba's Devotion series

Available in bookstores and online retailers.

Discover more great books at
CrossRiverMedia.com

An Unnatural Beauty

Holiness is not an endless list of "thou shalt nots." It's not how we behave, what we think, or how we react or respond to life and the people around us. You'll discover foundational truths from Scripture, the path to a deeper, more intimate relationship with God, and why holiness can't be achieved through our own efforts. With relatable stories, Esther reminds us that Holiness is not a what, but a glorious Who, and He's inviting you to share in His divine nature.

M. ESTHER LOVEJOY

Unbeaten

Difficult times often leave Christians searching the Bible for answers to the most difficult questions— Does God hear me when I pray? Why isn't He doing anything? Author Lindsey Bell understands the struggle. As she searched the Bible for answers to these tough questions, her studies led her through the stories of biblical figures, big and small. She discovered that while life brings trials, faith brings victory. And when we rely on God for the strength to get us through, we can emerge *Unbeaten*.

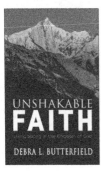

Unshakable Faith

With *Unshakable Faith*, you'll build an indestructible foundation to your faith and crush your doubts. This 7-week Bible study contains five to six lessons per week, each lesson designed to be completed in 20 minutes or less. Topics covered include your kingdom identity, faith fundamentals, your authority and power, and your weapons and armor. You'll grow and strengthen your faith, learn faith fundamentals, and learn to command the power and authority God has given you.

DEBRA L. BUTTERFIELD

GENERATIONS

What happens when God steps in to change one man's life?

Discover more great books at
CrossRiverMedia.com

THE GRACE IMPACT

The promise of grace pulses throughout Scripture. Chapter after chapter, the Bible shows a loving heavenly Father lavishing his grace on us through His son. In her book, The Grace Impact, author Nancy Kay Grace gives us a closer glimpse at God's character. His grace covers every detail of life, not just the good things, but the difficult, sad and complicated things. That knowledge can give us the ability to walk confidently through life knowing God is with us every step of the way.

MARRIAGE CONVERSATIONS

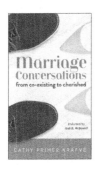

Marriage requires serious communication. So, we turn to the Master Communicator for strategies to soften hearts and strengthen resolve. Cathy will help you initiate practical, foundational truths; replace magical thinking with rock solid miraculous biblical truths; understand why we get married in the first place; and invigorate your closest relationship. Inspire the breathtaking relationship your heart is craving.

GROWING IN CHRIST

When Pauline and her husband, Tom sold their charter fishing boat and house in sunny Florida to move to a tobacco farm in North Carolina, they had a dream of growing their own food. They have experienced a few successes but mostly failures. However, God's economy is never wasted. He wove their mid-life-change-of-life into a tapestry of His grace.

Books that build battle-ready faith.

If you enjoyed this book, will you consider sharing it with others?

- Please mention the book on Facebook, Instagram, Pinterest, or another social media site.

- Recommend this book to your small group, book club, and workplace.

- Head over to Facebook.com/CrossRiverMedia, 'Like' the page and post a comment as to what you enjoyed the most.

- Pick up a copy for someone you know who would be challenged or encouraged by this message.

- Write a review on your favorite ebook platform.

- To learn about our latest releases subscribe to our newsletter at CrossRiverMedia.com.

Made in United States
North Haven, CT
14 September 2022

24109632R00117